WHAT SMART WOMEN KNOW

Also by Steven Carter and Julia Sokol

**WHAT REALLY HAPPENS IN BED
IS ANYONE OUT THERE?
HE'S SCARED, SHE'S SCARED**

WHAT SMART WOMEN KNOW

Steven Carter
and
Julia Sokol

A Dell Trade Paperback

Smart Women Know . . .
    No Woman Is Born Smart.

Smart Women Also Know . . .
    There Are Two Ways To Get Smart—
The Hard Way And The Easy Way.

Most smart women got smart the hard way, through first-hand experience. And they have the scars to prove it—painful memories of sleepless nights, tears, confusion, anger, self doubt and anxiety. Sure they have learned about life, love, and relationships, but they paid a high price for their wisdom.

We firmly believe that there is an easier way for a woman to get smart—an easier way to acquire the kind of information needed to handle relationships wisely without having to go through the traumatic events that often accompany the acquisition of such knowledge. How? Simply by listening to and learning from the experiences of other women. Wisdom without pain, understanding without heartache, insight without melodrama—that's what this book is all about.

The smartest women know that getting smart doesn't have to hurt.

A Smart Woman Knows That Her Most
Valuable Sense Is A Sense Of Self.

If a woman is to become smart, she has to understand what that means. Take Debra, for example. Even though Debra is intelligent, educated, creative, witty, and well organized, she is still not very smart about the way she leads her personal life. In fact, Debra would be the first to tell you that when she enters a relationship, there is a very good chance that she will "leave her brain" at the door. She says that there have been too many times in her life when she has lost sight of who she is and what she wants. Like many other women, Debra has learned that: a woman can be brilliant and still fail to be self-protective in her relationships; a woman can have a fabulously successful career and still be attracted to the wrong qualities in a man; a woman can be overwhelmingly talented and still not know how to be emotionally smart. Why is this so? Because being smart about life, love, and relationships is a lot different than being smart about nuclear physics.

So what are the basic qualities that make a woman truly smart and give her the best chances for personal and emotional happiness?

A Smart Woman Knows That Being Smart Means:

- staying rational.

- letting her intelligence control her emotions, not the other way around.

- trusting her values more than she trusts her hormones.

- choosing relationships that make her happy and allow her to grow.

- seeking out and accepting people who are positive and supportive.

- steering clear of relationships that spell out t-r-o-u-b-l-e.

- walking away from people who try to control her or cause her pain.

In a relationship, a smart woman knows that she needs to develop a realistic sense of what . . .

. . . she should give to a partner.

. . . what she can expect from a partner.

More important than anything, a smart woman never, ever, forgets that she is a whole person in her own right, with or without a man in her life.

Smart Women Know . . .
     Experience Is What You Get . . . When
You Don't Get What You Want.

Smart Women Know The Difference
Between . . .
. . . Sexy And Solid.
. . . Character And Charisma.
. . . Good Clothes And Good Values.
. . . Really Nice And Really Narcissistic.

Smart Women Know . . .

It's always a mistake to be so turned on by a man's style that you ignore his substance.

Victoria has just walked through the door at a large party. There are a great many people there, including at least a dozen eligible men. Within ten minutes, she spots an incredible-looking guy. Wow, she thinks, I could certainly be attracted to him. Close to six feet tall, with dynamite shoulders, he is wearing this really sharp jacket and a great-looking shirt. Everything about him appears interesting—good-looking, athletic, dynamic, exciting, maybe even rich, with a look that's sort of a cross between Kevin Costner and Dennis Quaid. There are two beautiful young women hanging around him trying to get his attention, and there is not a woman in the room who wouldn't want to go home with him. He has every reason to be sure of himself, and his body language tells the world that he knows it.

Within twenty minutes, Mr. Incredible and

Victoria make eye contact across the crowded room. Within thirty minutes, he is getting her a drink. Within an hour, he is asking her if he could meet her somewhere later. Victoria!!!!! *Stop Right Here!*

This is Victoria's pattern: She is only attracted to good-looking men with a touch of glamour, men who reek of sex appeal and charisma. Unless the guy looks like Warren Beatty, Mel Gibson, Pierce Brosnan, or Tom Selleck, he can forget it because she doesn't notice mere mortals. Victoria would tell you that this is because she is very picky and critical in her screening for Mr. Right. So why does Mr. Right always turn out to be Mr. Wrong?

That's easy. While it's true that Victoria is picky and critical, she is not picky and critical about the right things. She is so attracted to charisma and glamour that she doesn't stop to inquire about character. Character—that intangible quality that is reflected in a man's values and the way he treats the world and the women he's involved with—gets very short shrift.

This is interesting because although Victoria may look as though she is a member of the St. Tropez set, she herself is very solid. She has a solid job. She has solid friendships. She has a solid set of values. And what she wants from life is to bake cookies in a solid home with a solid family. So, as soon as the chemistry sparks between her and one of these glamour guys, she dons her apron and begins trying to turn Mr. Exciting into Mr. Homebody. A smart woman would advise Victoria that the chances of her pulling off this kind of alchemy are very slim.

Smart Women Know . . .

If a man acts as though he could have every woman in the room, he may eventually try to do just that.

If you want children, remember: Don Juan can afford to waste your time; he isn't punching a biological time clock.

The man who dresses like Arsenio Hall isn't hankering to be a homebody.

If he looks as though he spends more time shopping than you do, he will probably also expect more closet space.

ᔕᕼ

Glamorous, good-looking men are like delicate exotic houseplants—they need constant attention, and for that *maybe* you'll get flowers once a year.

ᔕᕼ

It will take more than a few moments of magic to transform a ladies' man into *your* man.

ᔕᕼ

When desperados ride off into the sunset, they ride off alone.

Smart Women Know . . .
    Obsessions Have No Real Place In A Smart Woman's Life.

At one time or another, every woman has been in the throes of an obsessive passion. Some women, totally grounded in reality, seem to be able to leave these types of feelings behind with adolescence. Others, equally sensitive, intelligent, and intuitive, specialize in them, nurture them and allow them to flourish and grow.

Which women are particularly vulnerable to obsessions? Any woman who has an unrealistic sense of expectations concerning love and togetherness. This can include those women with a rich fantasy life and a strong sense of drama and romance as well as those who come from backgrounds that provided no solid role models in terms of ordinary loving give and take.

What's wrong with obsessions? Nothing, if you don't mind being miserable three-quarters of the time. The problem is that obsessive love usually reflects a situation that is fraught with separations, feelings that aren't totally requited—or aren't requited in the way one wants—irreconcilable conflicts, and commitment anxieties. These are the elements that tend to make one obsessive, and they are also the elements that make for a terrible lifestyle.

Smart Women Know The Difference
Between . . .

. . . love and longing.

. . . yearning and enjoying.

. . . love and obsession.

. . . having a great passion and living a good life.

. . . going out to dinner and being out to lunch.

Stella has done it again. All the elements are in place. Out-of-sight sex, exquisite anticipation, the depths of despair, horrific arguments that have no solutions, agonizing separations, sweet reconciliations, tortured conversations, a full cast of bit players, etc., etc. Yes, Stella is in the throes of an *OBSESSION*.

This is not the first time Stella has been obsessed with someone, and it will probably not be the last. You see, Stella thinks love is about obsession. Consequently she lives a life of highs and lows, with few in-betweens. For Stella, grand passion certainly has its heady moments, but it's taking a terrific toll on her psyche, not to mention her digestive system.

Right now, Stella and her current obsession, Jack, are preparing for a trial separation for the summer. Jack told Stella that he is renting a summer house with friends. Stella will probably sit home, watch old movies on her VCR, wonder what Jack is doing, and sob. She will also spend several long weekends visiting her friends Denise and Howie at their country house. While there, she will review all the details between her and Jack. She'll ask Denise's advice. Howie's too. She probably won't pay any attention to what they say to her. She thinks they are sweet, but that they don't really understand. "How could they?" she asks herself.

Denise, who is Stella's "oldest" friend, has been married to Howie for five years; they have a two-year-old daughter. Denise says, "For as long as I've known Stella, she always gets involved with creeps." The first time Stella told Denise about Jack, Denise knew he was "trouble." He seemed too "smooth" to her. Besides, he was thirty-six, and he had never been able to make a commitment to anyone or anything. Denise can't understand why Stella thought he was going to be any different with her. Unless Stella is willing to look for and accept a "normal" guy—someone a little less "interesting" and more down to earth, Denise doesn't think Stella's life will ever improve. Stella tells Denise that she wishes she could meet someone like Howie, but Denise doesn't believe her. She's convinced that if Stella ever did come across another Howie, she wouldn't "have the sense to appreciate him."

If truth be told, Stella thinks that Howie is sweet, but uninteresting, and that Denise and Howie have a boring life, without passion. When Stella comes to visit, she enjoys it all—she likes going shopping with Denise and the baby on Saturday afternoons while Howie plays tennis or watches a ball game. She likes getting the paper with Howie and the baby on Sunday morning while Denise sleeps late. She likes taking a picnic and going to the lake with the whole family. She enjoys feeling morally superior when Denise and Howie have small squabbles about what's for dinner or who dented the car. She thinks it's all comfortable and cozy, but a trifle too dull and boring. If she ever gets married, she thinks it will never be like this. She isn't sure exactly what it is that she does want, but she knows she doesn't want anything so mundane.

Smart Women Know . . .

Comfortable, cozy, boring, and mundane are all part of a normal life and a normal relationship; these are the kinds of adjectives a smart woman wants in her life.

Dramatic, agonizing, tortured, convoluted, irreconcilable, horrific, and obsessive are words that belong on the jacket of a novel that you carry to the beach; a smart woman doesn't want to have these adjectives used to describe her *own* life.

If you think your friends "just don't understand" what's so special about your relationship, you had better take a closer look . . . they may understand more than you do. In fact, sometimes friends, who know you and love you, can have a much clearer perspective on what you're going through than you do.

If you find that you are spending an excessive amount of time *alone*, lying on the couch daydreaming or sobbing or both, you're not in love . . . you're obsessed.

If you find yourself constantly in turmoil, worrying about the details of your relationship, looking for cues and clues to help you understand what's happening, then you're not in love—you're obsessed.

Real long-term love can feel just as wonderful as the unending roller coaster of passion and pain . . . and you'll also have better vacations.

Letting go of an obsessive love is never going to be painless, but the sooner you do it, the sooner you can start healing.

An obsession can, and will, waste years of a woman's life.

Obsessions can, and will, cause headaches, gastrointestinal disturbances, palpitations, anxiety attacks, gray hair, and wrinkles.

More often than not, obsessive love is addictive, and it needs to be approached in the same way one would approach any other addiction—with a determination for recovery.

Recovering from a pattern of addictive, obsessive love relationships requires will power, professional help, and group support.

Smart Women Know . . .

God Created Dating So That A Woman Could Discover The Bad News About A Man *Before* She Gets Involved With Him, Not After.

Sally really hates dating. So do most of her friends. Just the mention of the word "dating" conjures up images of a thousand and one nights of self-consciousness, embarrassment, repulsion, bad restaurants, and awkward good-byes. And those are the good memories.

Sally definitely needs to develop a better attitude towards the dating experience. What she needs to know is that even though she is eager for the dating to end and the real relationship to begin, there is a very positive side to those brutal preliminaries. For dating is Sally's opportunity to do some careful investigating that will help her decide whether or not a particular man has long-term potential, short-term potential, or no potential at all. A smart woman knows that few women use dating to their advantage. Either they are so disinterested that they never give a guy a chance, or they are so attracted that their sense of judgment flies out the window.

A smart woman knows that dating requires caution, judgment, and common sense; she knows she shouldn't be too quick to reject a man just because there is no immediate chemistry. Sometimes she just needs to know him better, and the chemistry can change. A smart woman also knows that she should never be so blinded by lust that she fails to pay attention to any of the following:

- his attitude towards women in general
- his attitude towards money
- his attitude towards his family
- his attitude towards his career
- his attitude towards his car
- his attitude towards *your* career
- his ability to share
- his ability to play fair
- his ability to laugh

- his ability not to take himself too seriously

- his ability to take himself seriously enough

- his addictions (smoking, drinking, drugs, etc.)

- his potential aversions (your pets, your taste, your friends, your religion, anchovies, etc.)

- his politics

- his religious beliefs

- his values

- his neuroses

- his history with women

Smart Women Know . . .

Dating is something you do to find out whether or not you want to get involved with a man . . . so take your time.

Smart Women Know . . .

Your first dinner date in a restaurant is more than just a meal; it's a microcosm of what life would be like with this person.

It's your first big date, and often that means dinner. Pay attention, and you will receive an extraordinary amount of information. The first evening out will provide clues and cues of the kind of behavior you can expect in the next week, the next year, or the next decade . . . should the relationship continue.

Keeping this in mind, and also keeping in mind the fact that everyone has his bad days, and bad habits, a smart woman knows that before she starts fantasizing about a lifetime of meals, she should think twice about:

- any man who flirts with anyone other than you, including, but not limited to, the coat-check girl, the waitress, or the waiter.

- any man who asks you to meet him in a restaurant and then is more than ten minutes late.

24

- any man who won't share anything.

- any man who eats everything with his fingers.

- any man who won't eat anything with his fingers.

- any man who doesn't at least *offer* to pay for the entire meal.

- any man who gets angry if you offer him money.

- any man who chooses an expensive restaurant and then expects you to pay for half.

- any man who chooses an expensive restaurant and then won't order wine because it's too expensive.

- any man who orders an expensive wine without consulting you and then expects you to pay for half.

- any man who invites you to dinner and then doesn't have any money to pay the bill.

- any man who figures your share of the bill with a calculator.

- any man who changes tables more than once.

- any man who changes his order more than once.

- any man who sends his food back more than once.

- any man with major "food rules."

- any man who won't mix food groups (protein with carbohydrates, milk with fruit) because he's trying to get "fit for life."

- any man who wears his napkin like a bib.

- any man who stiffs the waiter.

- any man who mentions any bodily fluid during dinner.

- any man who asks if bread costs extra.

- any man who fights with the waiter.

- any man who drinks too much.

- any man who keeps getting ketchup in his hair.

- any man who gets soup in his beard, and leaves it there.

- any man who tries to control you by telling you what to order or how to eat it.

- any man who won't tell you what he's ordering until it's too late to change your mind.

- any man who won't check your coat because it costs a dollar.

- any man who pays more attention to what is going on at the other tables than he does to you.

- any man who only makes eye contact with his food.

- any man who eats all of his meal, plus half of yours.

- any man who tells you he always orders the same thing, no matter where he eats.

- any man who says he is allergic to half the things you order.

- any man who examines all the glasses and silverware for dirt or germs.

- any man who lets the check sit on the table too long.

- any man who makes a face when he looks at the bill.

- any man who looks at the menu and begins talking excessively about his fears concerning one of the following: aflatoxin, botulism, worms, pesticides, Agent Orange or other herbicides, alar, sulfites, aluminum, or lead.

- any man who is inappropriately sexual during dinner.

- any man who won't talk about himself.

- any man who talks only about *himself, his* life, and *his* interests.

- any man who appears completely disinterested in listening to anything about *you, your life* or *your* interests.

A Smart Woman Knows The Difference
Between . . .
. . . Marriageable And Married.
. . . Intimacy And Seduction.
. . . A Real Relationship And A Real Con
Job.
. . . Someone Who Is Going To Leave His
Wife and Someone Who Already Has.

Smart Women Know . . .

All of the good ones may be taken, but so are many of the bad ones.

Stacey has only known Alan a couple of weeks, and she likes him . . . a lot. She thinks he's very open and sensitive. Unlike other men she's known, Alan is attentive, affectionate, and doesn't appear afraid of intimacy. He seems to like her a lot too. In fact he likes her so much that he says he wants to take her with him on his next business trip, which just happens to be a week-long conference in Hawaii. He says he wants to have a "real" relationship with her. Stacey knows that this means he wants to sleep with her. She wants to sleep with him, too.

There's only one problem—Alan is married. He says it's no longer a "real" marriage. Stacey thinks that means he no longer sleeps with his wife. Alan says his wife "has her own life," and that he doubts that she would care, even if she knew. She might even be "grateful that he's out of her hair." Why are they still together? Alan says "real estate," "kids," and "guilt."

Stacey is very torn. On the one hand, Alan and Hawaii; on the other, Alan's wife and family. She isn't sure what she should do.

Smart Women Know . . .

Married

A week in Hawaii isn't worth one single weekend of imagining your lover having a backyard barbecue with the wife and kids while you are at home waiting and hoping for the phone to ring.

If a married man is genuinely interested, he'll be just as interested after he leaves his wife . . . which is the only time you should even consider dating him.

A line such as "she has her own life" is the 90s version of "my wife doesn't understand me."

Once you get involved with a married man, you may wish you "had your own life" as well.

≈

If his wife doesn't understand him, you probably won't understand him either.

≈

If he implies that his wife doesn't like sex, or doesn't like him, you should realize that she probably has her reasons.

≈

Married men sometimes use the nearest available single woman to help ease the pain of exiting from a marriage; once the marriage is finished, so is the relationship.

≈

It's an old saying, but it's true: If a man is able to deceive his wife, chances are he will be able to deceive you too.

≈

When things get serious, married men have been known to hide behind their wives to fend off the "other woman."

≈

When a man says he is staying with a marriage because of "real estate," "kids," and "guilt," it usually means he is totally dependent on his wife.

Married men who go out with other women are like oysters: One in a million has something precious inside, the rest are just slimy.

Some men always have affairs: They get off on the danger of being caught.

A Smart Woman Knows She's Not Being
Smart When:
• She Thinks Having A Bad Relationship Is
Better Than Being Alone.
• She Needs A Man To Validate Her Sense
Of Worthiness.
• She Puts Her Life On "Hold" Until The
Day She Has A Committed Relationship.
• She Can't Find Joy In Beaches, Music,
Sunsets, Movies, Shopping, Cooking—
Anything—Unless There Is A Man To Share
It.
• She Forgets That Having A Relationship
Can Create As Many Problems As It Solves.
• She Thinks She Needs A Man To Make
Her Feel Special.

Smart Women Know . . .
A Sense Of Self Means Knowing What You Have To Offer And Not Offering It Too Quickly.

Most people think Linda is really something. After all, she has a terrific education, she runs her own business, she's very attractive, and she has a hundred and one enviable talents. Here's a list of some of the things Linda knows how to do: She can hang wallpaper, put up drywall, fix a leaky faucet, and upholster furniture; she can do her own taxes, make killer pasta sauce, read while she rides her exercise bike, cable-knit a sweater, and tell you the top scorer on every team in the NBA. Linda, who is divorced with a ten-year-old son, is a wonderful mother, a good friend, and a superlative cook. In short, Linda is Wonder Woman and Super Woman rolled into one. But Linda thinks that, by herself, she is nothing. Unless she has a man around to tell her that she is beautiful, smart, and talented, Linda feels dreadful. Although she doesn't admit it very often, without a man, Linda doesn't feel as though she has a life.

If a man shows even the slightest interest in pursuing her, or if he does, or says, something that makes her feel beautiful, desirable, and important, she jumps right in. It's not that she wants to be involved with creeps, but her lack of self-esteem and judgment are controlling factors in her life. That's how she ends up with men who don't deserve her. She is so anxious to be part of a couple that she is too quickly sold on the man. It seems as though her eyes are almost totally closed. Consequently, who can keep track of all of Linda's ex-boyfriends? . . .

There was Michael, who was always about to leave his wife, but never did; George, who was always about to leave his office, but never did; Fred, who found fault with everything about her —from the way she talked and walked to the way she drove her car; Harry, who hit on all her friends; Ted, who spent more time with his tennis partner than he did with her. She also tried to develop relationships with Edward, who never talked; Alan, who never shut up; Bob, who never showed up; and Barney, who always showed up stoned.

Smart Women Know . . .

Low self-esteem can often lead even the most extraordinary women into destructive relationships.

Self-esteem is not just a 90s catch phrase; it is the core of any positive relationship you will ever have.

If you are always involved with Mr. Wrong, you may never get the opportunity to meet Mr. Right.

It's not smart to let down the drawbridge for every man who claims he's your knight in shining armor.

A Smart Woman Knows That Mr. Right Isn't Always Mr. Obvious.

Women are always getting angry at men who fail to get beyond the superficial. They complain that the average guy walks into a room, and—who does he notice and what does he notice? Typically, it's the prettiest woman, the shortest skirt, the most flamboyant outfit, what's on the television, and what's to eat.

But some women do the same thing. There are wonderful men walking the streets, but they aren't always the ones who stand out in the crowd. As a matter of fact, much of the time, they specifically *don't* stand out in the crowd. That doesn't mean that a good man has to be boring and ordinary. It just means that it takes time to see the ways in which he is fascinating and special.

Sometimes the only clue that you have that a man is genuine and sincere is that he doesn't appeal to any of your romantic fantasies:

- He doesn't need to be saved.

- He doesn't need help in finding himself.

- He isn't overwhelmingly good-looking.

- He isn't spectacularly rich.

- He isn't totally driven and consumed by ambition.

- He isn't completely macho.

- He doesn't have a major fatal flaw that needs mending.

- He isn't totally interesting or intriguing.

- He doesn't say the kinds of romantic things you dream of hearing—at least not until he's known you for a very long time.

A Smart Woman Knows How To Tell The Good Guys From The Bad Guys.

Finding a good man is sort of like trying to find a parking space in New York City. The best ones always seem to be taken, and while a lot of others look good from a distance, when you get up close, there's always a fire hydrant or a yellow line. But with both parking spaces and good men, they can eventually be found; if you don't give up, it's simply a matter of time.

Barbara Smith's husband, Tom, is a good man. Why? Because Tom is a real man. He does things that real men do, and those things are not that different from the things that real women do. When a woman talks to him, he listens and tries to understand what he is being told. When he feels threatened, he acknowledges it. When he was single, and he went to bed with a woman for the first time, his hands would sweat. He's made nervous by a variety of life situations, and he knows he is nervous, and he knows that being nervous is okay. He doesn't try to control or ma-

nipulate the women he knows to get what he
wants. He never has. Now that he's married, he's
utterly devoted to Barbara, and completely supportive of her needs. He thinks about what's best
for her, he wouldn't dream of being unfaithful,
and his marriage is as important to him as it is to
his wife. In short, Tom is a sincere good guy.

How do you recognize a man like Tom Smith
if you meet him for the first time; how would you
know he was a "good guy"? It's true, Tom doesn't
have "sincere" tatooed on his forehead, but he
does have it permanently etched in his personal-
ity and his behavior. In fact, if you met a Tom,
you might not give him the kind of time and
thought he deserves. Why? Because he's not neu-
rotic enough to intrigue you; he's not evasive
enough to titillate you; he's not handsome enough
to overwhelm you; and he's not charming enough
to sweep you off your feet. He certainly doesn't
have a series of practiced moves that makes for
polished seduction. Yes, he may be very romantic,
he may even send flowers, but usually after he
falls in love, not when he's trying to make you fall
in love. Yes, he may bring you wonderful gifts, but
on your second anniversary, not on your second
date.

The fact is that when you meet a "good guy",
his hat doesn't give him away . . . nor does the

color of his clothes. But a "good guy" has most, if not all, of the following:

A "good guy" has a realistic lifestyle.
> He has a real home, real work, real bills, real pets, real family, and a real way of dealing with all of them.

A "good guy" has realistic goals.
> This man may not want to conquer the world, but he will want to maximize his potential and be the best he can be.

A "good guy" is attracted to women who reflect his values and interests.
> This man has the sense to stay away from grand obsessions and focuses on women with whom he can have an easy relationship. In short, he doesn't spend his life trying to prove that oil and water can mix.

A "good guy" wants an equal partner he can share things with.
> This man doesn't want a relationship in which one partner is overly dependent or completely dominating.

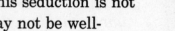

*A "good guy" doesn't try to
manipulate or use a woman.*

This man is not going to sweep you
off your feet so he can steal your
shoes. Because his seduction is not
rehearsed, it may not be well-
choreographed, but that's its appeal.

*A "good guy" is supportive without
being controlling.*

This man wants his partner to feel
happy and fulfilled, and he wants to
help her achieve her goals.

*A "good guy" knows how to listen to a
woman speak.*

This man is not so egomaniacal that
he can only focus on *his* problems
and *his* point of view.

*A "good guy" is fair, and he knows
how to share responsibilities.*

This man knows how to do the
laundry, make the beds, and cook the
dinner, and he insists upon doing his
share.

44

A "good guy" is honest.
This man tries to deal with
everything truthfully including his
feelings, his fears, and his needs.

≈

*A "good guy" doesn't have
unreasonable boundaries.*
This man doesn't make you feel bad
by excluding you from meaningful
parts of his life, and he doesn't have
unreasonable rules about how far he
will go in the relationship or how
close he will allow you to get.

≈

*A "good guy" is capable of
commitment.*
This man wants to have a solid,
sharing, committed relationship, and
he has a lifestyle that reflects his
ability to form permanent
attachments.

≈

A "good guy" is well intentioned.
This man always wants what is best
for both of you.

A Smart Woman Has The Good Sense To Appreciate A Man Who:

• Allows A Relationship To Grow Slowly.
• Doesn't Push The Development Of Sexual Intimacy.
• Is Grounded In Reality, Not Fantasy.
• Knows What Love Is, Knows What Long-Term Commitment Is, And Doesn't Take Either Of Them Lightly.
• Doesn't Make Promises Until He Knows He Will Keep Them.
• Knows How To Develop A Relationship Without Relying On Brooding Love Poems, Tortured Phone Calls, Inappropriate Gifts, Lavish Entertainment, Or Soulful Confessions.

Smart Women Know . . .

Any man who falls in love quickly can fall out of love just as quickly.

Cheryl met Gary on a blind date. At first she wasn't sure he was her type. But it didn't take long for Gary to convince her otherwise. On the very first date, he made it clear how "special" he thought she was. The next day he sent a poem and a dozen roses. By the end of the first week, he said he thought he was "falling in love with her."

Gary is so intense that Cheryl is spinning from it all. From the time she was a little girl, Cheryl has dreamed about a man responding to her as passionately as Gary is. He seems to be completely overwhelmed by his feelings. He phones several times a day; he brings her silly extravagant presents; he wants to see her every night, even though it means his driving more than a hour each way; he talks about what they will do together, in the future; he envelops her with a sense of intimacy and acceptance.

Cheryl has been terribly flattered by all this;

hearing Gary's words of love makes her feels won-derful—wanted and desirable. But the pace is scaring her; everything seems to be happening so fast. It's like something out of a romance novel. One voice inside her is saying "be careful," but another is saying, "go with it . . . it could be the big one." Which voice should she listen to?

Smart Women Know . . .

It takes a long time for real love to build. Two weeks is not a long time. Neither is two months.

The man who is skillful at conducting whirl-wind courtships has probably had lots of practice.

The words "I love you" do not roll easily or quickly off the tongue of a sincere man.

A man who isn't shy about saying "I love you" has probably said it to too many women.

A man who is very romantic at the beginning of a relationship is sometimes taking a vacation in fantasyland; when he returns to earth, he could come crashing down on your heart.

❧

You have nothing to lose by slowing a man down. If it's going to be the relationship of the century, you'll have a century to enjoy it.

❧

Slowing a relationship down does not mean rejecting the man; it means talking about your fears, taking it slow, and discussing everything so you are both clear about what you mean.

❧

It's not smart to start planning the honeymoon until you are sure that "I love you" means the same thing to him as it means to you.

A Smart Woman Has The Sense To
Appreciate A Man Who:
• Gives You Heartburn From His Cooking,
Not His Behavior.
• May Be A Little Boring, But At Least
Doesn't Talk About Himself Constantly.
• Disagrees With You About Day-To-Day
Decisions—Which Movies To See, Which
Vegetables To Have With Dinner—Not
Whether Or Not He Should Try To Sleep
With Your Best Friend.
• Runs Out Of Things To Say, But Doesn't
Care.
• Isn't Always Checking Up On You.
• Has Tedious Everyday Problems Such As
Root Canals And Tennis Elbow—As
Opposed To All-Consuming Psychological
Conflicts That Even Freud Couldn't Analyze.
• Pays His Bills On Time.
• Has A Receding Hairline And Doesn't
Worry About It.
• Wants To Meet Your *Whole* Family, Not
Just Your Good-Looking Sister.

Smart Women Know . . .

. . . the difference between a potential husband and a potential disaster.

Every woman past the age of twenty has known her share of weirdos . . . some she's dated, some she's gotten involved with, and some she may even have lived with—or, as bad luck would have it, married. Rhonda is no exception. In fact, Rhonda has had more than her share of weirdos—she's had several shares. There was Zack the anarchist, Edward the geneticist, Philip the oncologist, Carlos the soccer player, Raymond the performance artist, and William the con artist. And those were the ones she didn't marry. Twice, she was not so lucky.

If Rhonda had any psychic energy left in her soul right now, she would want to warn every woman on the planet to learn from her mistakes. She has paid a hefty price to become smart, but she now knows that it doesn't have to be that way. That's because a smart woman knows to think twice and ask a lot of questions before getting more seriously involved with any man who:

- uses Murine and nasal spray more often than you use lipstick.

- roots for the bad guys on Miami Vice.

- boasts that his boat can outrace a coast guard cutter.

- thinks the Marquis de Sade had an "interesting" outlook on life.

- is convinced he was once an eleventh-century warrior.

- tries to hypnotize you.

- has children who refuse to see him.

- has children whom he never wants to see.

- pays cash for everything.

- has lifetime subscriptions to *Soldier of Fortune* and *Marine Sniper.*

- wants to send you to his plastic surgeon or remake you in any way, shape, or form.

- has more creditors than he has friends.

- has more ex-wives and live-ins than you have party dresses.

- knows all the casino dealers by their first names.

- tries to borrow money from you, and all your friends.

- tries to control you in any way.

- tries to get you involved in sexual behavior you dislike.

- reads *The Satanic Verses* on public transportation.

- changes residences more often than you change your sheets.

- still talks about joining the Peace Corps.

- won't tell you what he does for a living.

- doesn't let you visit his home.

- never stops talking about the ex-wife, or ex-girlfriend, he *"really* hates."

- has told so many lies that he gets his "stories" mixed up.

- doesn't speak to anyone in his family.

- has a bookie who is out to get him.

A Smart Woman Knows The Difference Between Being "Special" And Being Just Another Victim.

We all like to think we are a little special, a little different from everybody else. And we are. And it's important that we never forget that each of us has special talents and special charm and special value. But sometimes this sense of knowing she's different from everybody else is what makes a woman believe that it's "going to be different" with her. A woman needs to realize that a really bad guy ultimately is a really bad guy. He's been unkind to the women in his past, and he will almost certainly be unkind to her.

A Smart Woman Doesn't Blame The Women In A Man's Past Until She Has All The Facts.

Smart Women Know . . .

Even though you may be the right woman, the wrong man will still be the wrong man.

Ellen likes to think of herself as an intelligent, caring, giving woman. And she is. From the time she was a little girl, she has heard people refer to specific difficult men saying, "he hasn't met the right woman yet." In all of her relationships, Ellen has tried to be the right woman. A part of her honestly believes that if she is good enough, accepting enough, giving enough, she will be rewarded with the love of a difficult man.

Right now Ellen is trying very hard to get over Ted, who broke her heart. Before Ted broke Ellen's heart, he broke Janet's heart. Before he broke Janet's heart, he broke Anne's heart. Before he broke Anne's heart, he broke Jessica's heart. So why did Ellen think it would be any different with her?

When Ellen met Ted, he was still in the process of ending it with Janet, who he said was creating scenes and making him "crazy with her phone calls." Ted explained that he and Janet had been mismatched, but he felt guilty for letting the relationship continue as long as it did. A mutual friend told Ellen that Ted had devastated Janet and someone else pulled Ellen aside at a party, telling her to watch out, that Ted was a killer with women. Ellen wasn't surprised. Ted himself had told her that he had a terrible history with women. In fact, he said, sometimes he wondered whether he would ever be capable of a "normal" emotional life. However Ted also told Janet-stories that made Ellen believe that all of the women he had known had serious problems, or were somehow deficient. And he had terrible stories to tell about women. One girlfriend had been so out of control that she emptied the contents of his kitchen cabinets out onto the floor. Another still called him every night at midnight and hung up the phone the second he answered. Still another—two years after the split up—saw him in a restaurant with another woman and came over and made a scene.

Ellen believed that she was different, that she was special to him, and Ted reinforced that belief. He told her that she was the most loving, giving woman he had ever known. That's why Ellen didn't pay enough attention to Ted's history. She analyzed Ted's problem by telling herself that he had never tried to have a relationship with the right woman. Of course she thought she was the right woman. She thought they had the right relationship, and she believed that everything would be different with her.

And for a while it was. They had so much in common that they agreed about most things, and everything seemed almost magical . . . until the day Ted stopped treating Ellen as if she were special and began treating her exactly as he had treated the other women in his life. Within a couple of months, Ted was telling someone else she was special, and Ellen—like Janet before her—was making scenes that were making Ted crazy.

Smart Women Know . . .

If you think he's going to be any different with you than he was with any other woman, then you're not being very smart.

If he tells you that his ex-wife tried to run him over, the day will probably come when you will wish she had.

No matter how wonderful you are, there are some men out there who can make you, and any other woman, crazy—these are not men you should worry about losing.

A Smart Woman *Believes* Any Man Who Tells Her . . .

. . . He Has A Problem With Commitment.

. . . He's Never Really Loved Anybody.

. . . He May Be Moving Away Soon.

. . . His Ex-Wife Or Ex-Girlfriend Has Reasons To Hate Him.

. . . He Hasn't Found Himself.

. . . He Found Himself, But He Doesn't Like What He Found.

. . . He Has Trouble Settling Down To A Steady Job.

. . . He Needs A Team Of Therapists To Keep Him Functional.

A Smart Woman Knows . . .

If you are truly serious about settling down, you should stop hanging out at the airport.

Sarah says she wants to get married. She says it is the one thing that is really missing from her life, and she really wants a husband and children. Really. But Sarah's friends are beginning to wonder about what Sarah really wants.

For someone who says she needs nothing more than one stable man to happily settle down with, you would never know it from the guys she dates. You see, Sarah has never been involved with a vine-covered-cottage type, except for the ones who are already living in vine-covered cottages with their wives. Let's take a quick look at some of Sarah's relationships.

Sarah met Jonathan one week, to the day, before he was to leave on his "self discovery" trip to Nepal. He was wildly romantic, and she fell madly in love and began to think about the life they could have together. She even became a vegetarian. Two years, two postcards, and 730 bowls of brown rice later, Sarah decided she'd better start looking for someone else.

Sarah met Andrew on an airplane. He was wildly romantic and sent her three dozen roses and a book of poetry. She was smitten, but he was smut. You see, Andrew was married, and his wife was pregnant with their third child. Because Andrew lived two thousand miles away, Sarah didn't find out that Andrew's wife was pregnant until after the child was born. That's when Sarah became hysterical. And that's when Andrew broke it off, saying he needed time to think the whole thing through. Andrew is still thinking. . . . Watch Andrew think. . . . Think, Andrew, think.

Sarah and Steven met at a party. Steven was single, Steven lived in the same town, Steven was available. Well, sort of. He *was* single, and he wasn't involved with anyone. But he warned Sarah, straight out, that he wasn't interested in marriage. He openly acknowledged that his friends thought he was commitmentphobic. In fact he had never gone out with anyone for longer than two months. He told Sarah the honest truth about that too. But boy did he pursue Sarah. He was so wildly romantic that Sarah was sure she would be the exception. She wasn't.

Sarah had barely recovered from Steven when she met Tony. He was, as you will probably guess by now, also wildly romantic. Tony acknowledged that his personal history was a mess. Married at twenty-one, he had left his first wife for another woman at twenty-four. At twenty-six, he left that woman when he met his second wife. She left him when he was thirty. Since then he had been living, off and on, with another woman, but he told Sarah that it was no longer "very serious." However within weeks he began breaking dates with Sarah and seemed less accessible. Now he tells Sarah that he isn't sure "what he wants." Sarah, of course, is sure of one thing: When he is not with her, he is still seeing the woman with whom it was no longer serious. Sarah is very unhappy, but the relationship continues in this fashion.

Smart Women Know . . .

Any man who doesn't know "what he wants" doesn't deserve what he has.

❧

The man who is heading for Khatmandu to find himself is going to get rid of any women he meets on the way.

❧

Any man who is "looking for himself" isn't looking for a wedding band.

❧

If you want to settle down, you would be wise to steer clear of cowboys, racecar drivers, would-be riverboat gamblers, and anyone else who likes living on the edge.

❧

If a man is wildly romantic at the beginning of the relationship, chances are he is wildly unrealistic and totally undependable.

❧

If you want a steady, dependable relationship, you've got to find a steady, dependable man.

Smart Women Know It's Time To End The
Relationship When:
• He Makes You Feel Bad More Often Than
He Makes You Feel Good.
• Your Fear Of Losing Him Is Making You
Disregard All Your Realistic Needs.
• His Behavior Is Chipping Away At Your
Self-Esteem.
• You Tell Him How Sad Or Upset You Feel,
But He Makes No Attempt To Change
What He Is Doing.
• He Stops Trying To Please You.
• You Have A Better Time Remembering
The Past Than You Do Living In The
Present.
• His Behavior Is Making You Realistically
Jealous.
• He Starts Telling You That He Needs
"More Space."

Smart Women Know . . .

. . . the difference between being in love and being in pain.

Margaret met Paul in November at a party. She was dancing with someone else when she saw Paul standing in a corner of the room, staring at her as though he was a drowning man and she was a lifejacket he didn't know how to reach. Finally when she was getting a drink, he walked over and introduced himself. He seemed so shy, so worried about whether or not she would like him. As it turned out, however, it took her only a very short time to realize that she was wild about him. The first few weeks of the relationship were like a romantic haze. Margaret was deliriously happy. She couldn't stop telling her friends how privileged she felt, and when she thought about her good fortune, she was overwhelmed. Paul was attractive, desirable, charming, intelligent, and obviously adored her. What could be wrong?

Then suddenly Paul changed. At first it was subtle. He didn't call quite as often, and he seemed to be retreating. Initially Margaret thought it was just a phase that she expected Paul to get over. Then it became more serious. Paul started talking about "seeing other people," about "needing space"—and he was less available to her. When they were together, it was still wonderful. That's why Margaret had a hard time accepting what was happening—until Paul began to be really hurtful. He started openly flirting with other women, and excluding her from his plans.

There was no way around it—Paul was backing away. That's when Margaret started crying in earnest. It has been almost six months, and the relationship definitely has more pain than gain. For every good hour that they have been together, there has been a bad day during which Paul has done something to make Margaret feel confused, hurt, and lonely. For every tender moment during which he tells her he cares about her and doesn't want to hurt her, there is a miserable weekend during which he leaves her alone, wondering where he is, and what he is doing. For every intimate exchange, there are five agonizing encounters when he seems he to be detached. Margaret says she is in love with Paul, but when you do the math, how can it all add up?

Margaret always remembers the beginning, and the way Paul looked at her. She keeps thinking that what is happening is some sort of nightmare or test—that soon Paul will wake up, and things will go back to the way they were at the beginning, when he was pursuing her.

Right now, Paul says he is confused. He says he doesn't know what he wants. He says he may be too immature to love anybody. He says he doesn't deserve Margaret's love. But he also indicates that he is very jealous, that he would be deeply hurt if Margaret went out with anyone else, that he feels closer to her than to anyone else. Sometimes they have awful scenes during which Margaret finds herself screaming at Paul, or almost pleading with him. But her sadness or hysteria does not change what Paul does.

Margaret believes Paul loves her. She thinks he is simply conflicted but that it will all work out. She thinks if she waits long enough, and is a model of virtue and understanding, everything will be okay. But it's not easy. She has a whole range of emotions—anger, anxiety, grief. Her parents and friends have noticed that she is miserable, but Margaret doesn't want them to know how bad it has gotten, so she makes excuses for Paul. Most of the time when he isn't available, she stays home; sometimes she watches television, sometimes she talks on the phone to friends. Most of the time, she cries.

Smart Women Know . . .

Crying is for weddings and funerals . . . not for Saturday nights.

There is a world of difference between his going through a phase and your being phased out.

Continue to love someone who is hurting you and, eventually, you will no longer love yourself.

Jealousy is an inaccurate barometer of a man's feelings or intentions.

A lifeguard's warning: If you try to save a drowning man, you run the risk of going down with him.

There is a limit to how much pain and confusion any man is worth.

∾∾

Anger + Anxiety + Grief ≠ Happiness.

∾∾

If it hurts, it probably isn't good for you.

A Smart Woman Has The Good Sense To
Appreciate A Man Who . . .
• Has No Interesting Problems.
• Feels Good About Himself.
• Feels Good About Where He Is In Life.
• Doesn't Draw Her Into His Psychodrama.
• Shows Up When He Says He'll Show Up.
• Doesn't Look Like A Wounded Animal.

Smart Women Know . . .

E-N-A-B-L-I-N-G is the wrong way to spell love.

M ary looks like she just stepped out of a yogurt ad, all apple-cheeked, cheery, and fit for life. She's the eternal optimist and, heaven knows, she has to be. You see, for reasons that her friends can't understand, she is perpetually involved with fatally flawed men . . . men who drink too much, men who gamble too much, men who dream too much, men who fight too much. Mary says that it isn't her fault that this type of man always "finds" her. Nonetheless, when they do, she thinks she can help them. And she believes that it is possible to build a life with them. Unfortunately, Mary's life is played out like a bad soap opera.

There was Paul who lost too much at the race track; Larry who had million-dollar dreams (and tastes) and hundred-dollar unemployment checks; Frank who left his heart (and certain relevant segments of his brain) in a bottle of Scotch; and

Gerry who fought with everyone including his many bosses, her friends (he didn't have any), his co-workers, and her family (his had stopped speaking to him years ago). What these men had in common was how they made Mary feel. For a time, each of them made her feel special, important, useful, and very, very needed.

Instead of dealing with any of these men realistically, Mary dreamed of a better tomorrow in which the problems would disappear, and she would have the fantasy relationship she had always imagined. Although Mary saw herself as saving these men, her actions actually encouraged their dependency. She listened to their problems, she spent long hours trying to sort out the details of their unhappy childhoods, and, in at least one instance, she ended up taking care of someone's invalid ex-wife. They drove her car, they ate her cooking, and, of course, they borrowed money. Mary thinks that she understands these men and what they have gone through. She sees herself as being strong enough to deal with their problems, and it's certainly true that she has "put up" with a lot from them, often including infidelity. Nonetheless, she likes hoping with them, loving them no matter what, working through their problems with them, and trying to get them to change.

It would be a mistake to assume that Mary's "saintly" behavior made any of these men love her more. It didn't. In fact, it frequently made them deeply resentful. Only one of them, Frank, actually did change, but within weeks after he became sober, the relationship changed as well. He needed Mary less, and she complained that he spent more time with his friends at AA than he did with her. It turned out that a sober Frank was not as romantic, or as "interesting," as a soused Frank.

As far as the other men have been concerned, eventually their problems became overwhelming, and even Mary couldn't handle them. What can we learn from Mary's experiences?

Smart Women Know . . .

If the wrong men keep finding you, then you are giving off the wrong signals.

A man's fatal flaws should be a turn-off, not a turn-on.

There is a difference between being caring and being co-dependent.

If you are always trying to "fix his problems," it's time to start looking at your own.

If you really want to spend your life dealing with other people's problems, you should become a social worker and get paid to do it.

Addictive personalities cannot be saved by the love of a good woman; they need rehabilitation programs, not understanding and chicken soup.

It's not smart to get involved with a man whose idea of a continental breakfast is a croissant and a bottle of wine.

What *Do* Smart Women Know About Sex And Dating?

Women ask about this all the time. They say, "What about sex on the first date?" What they really mean is what about having sex with someone before you have a relationship with him—when you know him well enough to know that you want to go to bed with him, but you don't know him well enough to know whether either of you has any expectations or responsibilities for each other. That can be the first date, second date, tenth date . . . whenever. When a woman asks this question, she usually is not asking about some of the real practical considerations such as safe sex or contraception, although they certainly deserve some thought.

What is typically concerning a woman about pre-relationship sex are the emotional ramifications, and these are much more complicated than the old saw about whether or not either of you will respect *anyone* in the morning.

Smart Women Know . . .

Before you go to bed with a man for the first time, you need sufficient information about who he is, what he is, and why he is.

Let's face it, no matter how worldly a woman is, she still wants to know who she is sleeping with; she wants to know for sure that he will call her again; she wants to know that he's who he says he is; she wants to know for sure whether or not he is married or in another serious relationship; she wants to know if he's stable, if he is sincere, if he really likes her. Acquiring this kind of information takes more than a couple of dates.

The minute you have sex with a man, there is a very good possibility that you will be more vulnerable to him than you were before.

Vulnerability is one of the components of intimacy, and intimacy is what makes a relationship special. But you don't want to put yourself in

a vulnerable position with anyone
until you know whether or not he
deserves your trust . . . and that
takes time.

✎

*Unfortunately it is possible to feel
total and complete lust for a total and
complete rat.*

Just because you are overwhelmingly
attracted to someone doesn't mean
that you should act on it. Waiting
until you know more about a man
will give you the opportunity to
evaluate more aspects of his
character, including those that might
turn you off.

✎

*Once you get caught up in a sexual
maelstrom with a new partner,
common sense concerns frequently
shift to a back burner.*

Good chemistry between a man and
woman is great. But the best
chemistry has been known to turn
bad when other things in the
relationship are off kilter. You need
time to know whether or not you
really are meant for each other;

otherwise you can end up stuck with each other.

✎

If a man is really interested in a woman, he doesn't mind waiting; in fact, often he prefers it.

Women sometimes express concern about whether or not a relationship will ever get off the ground if there is no sex at the beginning. There is no question that sex moves a relationship to new plateau, but A SMART WOMAN KNOWS THAT SHE DOESN'T WANT TO GET TO THAT NEW PLATEAU UNTIL SHE IS SURE THAT'S WHERE *SHE* WANTS TO BE.

Smart Women Have The Good Sense To
Appreciate A Man Who:
• Is Steady And Reliable.
• Has A Stable Life.
• Has A Real Place To Live.
• Doesn't Make You Feel As Though If You
Don't Grab Him That Second, He'll Be Gone.
• Isn't Totally Intriguing, But Is Totally
Dependable.
• Can Comfortably And Honestly Discuss All
The Aspects Of His Life.

A Smart Woman Knows . . .

Unless you have good connections at Interpol, think twice before dating an elusive man.

Nancy met George three weeks ago when he "picked her up" at the produce department of the local supermarket by asking her to help him find "the perfect canteloupe". Usually Nancy doesn't talk to strange men, but she was immediately attracted to George and impressed by his boyish sense of humor. He asked if he could call her, and gave her his phone numbers, too. It wasn't long before Nancy realized that George was different from any other man she had ever dated. The difference? He couldn't be reached by phone. The home number he gave her had been disconnected (which George later blamed on a telephone company "screw-up" he hadn't bothered to straighten out) and his "work" number turned out to be an answering service (because his work took him out of the office so much, he explained).

Nancy likes George and has already gone out

with him twice, but he is not reachable by phone, and this bothers her. Besides he seems generally hard to pin down—about everything. For example, she's not sure where he really works. Since they met in a supermarket, they have no friends in common, so Nancy can't confirm any of the facts about George—not that he gives her many to confirm. On their second date, George said he "forgot something," and he took her to an apartment he said was his. They were only there for a few minutes so Nancy couldn't really look around, but the apartment looked strange, as though nobody really lived in it. This all bothers her. Should it?

Smart Women Know . . .

A good man may be hard to find, but he shouldn't be hard to phone.

The man who says he has no home phone often has something to hide . . . like a girlfriend . . . or a wife.

The man who can't be reached easily is giving you a message. It is: *"You can't reach me!"*

Any man who is difficult to find is difficult to keep.

If you can't find him, lose him.

Smart Women Know . . .

When A Man Disappears Suddenly, With No Real Explanation, It Is Because There Is Something Wrong With Him, Not Because There Is Something Wrong With You.

It's happened to almost every woman. She meets a man. Something special happens between them. She likes him. She thinks he likes her. She begins to trust him. Then he starts acting weird. Sometimes he just stops calling altogether, and she never does find out why. Other times, a pattern develops—he disappears, he shows up, he has excuses, he disappears again, he resurfaces, he has more excuses. She gets confused. She wonders what happened, she thinks about what went wrong. Was it something she said, something she did, something she didn't say, something she didn't do? Whether it happens right after your first date or right before your first Christmas together, there is no good explanation for such behavior, but there is an appropriate way to deal with it.

A Smart Woman Knows That She Should Walk Away And Forget Any Man Who:
• Stops Calling.
• Doesn't Show Up When He Says He Will.
• Doesn't Call When He Says He Will.
• Cancels Plans At The Last Minute.
• Cannot Be Counted On To Do What He Says He Will.

Smart Women Know . . .

Any man who doesn't show up or call when he says he will isn't worth the paper your phone number is printed on.

Beverly met Jake at an industry trade show. The chemistry was instantaneous and within two weeks they had already seen each other six times.

When Jake kissed Beverly good-bye after their sixth date, he told her he would speak to her the following day, and maybe they could do something. Beverly waited all day for Jake to phone, but he never did. Finally at ten o'clock at night, she phoned him. No answer. She reached him an hour later. He said he had, "fallen asleep." He said that when he woke it was already "too late to plan anything." She must have called "while he was out getting a bite to eat." Beverly was so relieved to hear his voice that she didn't make a big deal out of it.

Then after they had been "together" for a month, Jake invited Beverly to join him for a Sunday family picnic in the country. He told her he would pick her up at nine a.m. At eleven, he phoned to say he was having "a few problems" and that he'd get back to her. It has now been three days since that last phone call. Beverly is confused and furious. If she doesn't hear from him by this evening her best friend is going to make a "sorry, wrong number" phone call to his house to make sure he's still breathing.

Beverly's friend, Annie, has also had a man disappear, and she is very, very upset. Two and a half weeks ago, Annie met a man through her job. He was from out of town and came into her office to see her boss.

Normally Annie likes to take the time to get to know someone, but the fact that Bill was only going to be in town for a few days influenced her. That and the fact that she found him irresistible. Well you guessed it. It was magic. Pure magic. They had dinner three nights in a row. Then on Saturday, they spent the day at the park. Saturday night after dinner, Bill came home with her. He didn't leave until Sunday afternoon—just in time to catch his plane.

During this time, Annie found out all about him. About his childhood, about his bad relationship with his parents, about his brother whom he adored. She also heard about his work problems and the difficulties that led to his divorce. He told her everything! They talked and talked and talked! What happened between them seemed unbelievable! He asked her to come visit him for her vacation; he told her he would be back in a month, and they would have more time together then; he told her he would call her the next day. Annie thought this was the beginning of a major relationship.

For two and a half weeks, Annie has been waiting for that phone call—but it hasn't happened. She is beside herself. Did she say something, did she do something? Was there something wrong with her sexually? Did he hate the way she looked, felt, acted? Was she too repressed? Was she not repressed enough? What happened?

More than anything else, both Beverly and Annie want an explanation. Here it is:

Smart Women Know . . .

Every woman has at least one story to tell about a man who disappeared or didn't show up when he was supposed to. No matter how unusual their circumstances or intricate their explanations, disappearing men are as common as field mice.

The man who vanishes into thin air is a magician. First he makes you feel like you're floating on air . . . then he does the old disappearing trick. If he reappears, he'll probably try to saw you in half . . . then, like Houdini, he'll disappear again.

When a man disappears like this, he is not lying half-dead in an alley somewhere crying out your name.

The disappearing man often reappears (miraculously) the moment you have gotten over him . . . or found another man.

You should have the good sense not to feel guilty about anything you might have said or done that you think might have precipitated a man's disappearance.

Every woman gets upset when a man suddenly disappears, even if she didn't like him that much to start out with. His behavior triggers and reinforces every primal childhood fear of abandonment.

శ్రీ

Men have been known to disappear at all stages of a relationship—immediately after an extraordinarily good and intimate first date, right after an idyllic vacation, right before the wedding.

శ్రీ

Men typically disappear because the relationship has gotten too close for comfort; some men disappear early in the relationship because they are already involved with another woman.

శ్రీ

A man will typically disappear because he feels that you are expecting "more" than he is prepared to give. Because he realizes that he gave you this expectation, he is too guilty to have an honest conversation.

శ్రీ

This is a fact! If a man disappears on you, the only appropriate reaction is relief that you were saved from getting more involved with a total creep.

A Smart Woman Has The Good Sense To Appreciate Those Times In Her Life When She Is Without A Relationship.

Smart Women Know . . . whether it's finishing your masters, finishing your first novel, finishing your floors, or finishing your chores, many important things in life are easier to accomplish when you can focus totally on yourself. That's when you can . . .

> . . . *strengthen your friendships.*
> An unattached woman has the time to appreciate and enjoy friends, both new and old, and those things she can do with them. Make plans with friends—beaches, concerts, movies, picnics.

> . . . *further your career.*
> Without a man, you have extra time, extra energy, and fewer personal

demands. Now is the time for advancement if that's what you want.

≈

. . . *find your hidden talents.*
Did you ever want to paint? Do it now. Did you ever dream of learning how to play the piano? Why not now?

≈

. . . *develop new interests.*
French? Italian? Sanskrit? Skiing? Body surfing? Sailing? Photography? Travel?

≈

. . . *find yourself.*
Being alone means you can be utterly self-involved. Whether you are searching for your inner child or the secrets of the universe, there is no one to account to but you.

≈

. . . *lose yourself.*
Take a walk in the woods, a bike ride through France, or go on a retreat in the mountains. It's your choice and your schedule.

≈

. . . *do life your way.*
You can go to sleep when you want, for as long as you want; you can eat

exactly what you want, when you want, and where you want; you can go where you want, when you want, with whom you want—and come back when you feel like it; you can see the movies and tv programs you want to see, lying in bed at three o'clock in the morning surrounded by a mound of peanut butter crackers, and nobody can say anything; you can decorate your house the way you want; you can fill your apartment with pets; you can spend your money on whatever you see fit. In short you don't have to reach compromises with anyone except yourself. *Make the most of it!*

A Smart Woman Has The Good Sense To
Slow A Relationship Down Until She Is Sure
That:
• She Is Ready.
• Her Dream Man Won't Turn Into Her Worst
Nightmare.
• The Relationship Is Grounded In Reality,
Not Fantasy.
• He Is Sincere.
• He Is Stable.
• He Is Serious.
• He Knows What Love Is.
• He Knows What Commitment Is.
• Both Of You Share Similar Values.

Smart Women Know . . .

It's not smart to let your fear of being alone cloud your judgment.

Ever since her separation from Jason, Dorothy has been overwhelmed with loneliness. When she comes home from work, the house seems empty and devoid of life. The first few minutes are always the toughest, especially in the winter when the sun has already set and she finds herself feeling the deserted atmosphere of the house. For a couple of weeks Dorothy relished being alone because she had gotten out of such a bad relationship, but now she seems to be spending more and more time thinking about how lonely she feels.

Dorothy has friends who say they are happy living alone, but she doesn't really believe these people. She doesn't know what to do with herself unless there is someone with her. Too many nights she finds herself staring at her apartment —at the vastness of her closets, all that extra space begging for a man's wardrobe; at her refrigerator, its twenty-one cubic feet filled only with a couple of Lean Cuisines and two pints of Haagen Dazs. Sure, friends, television, and telephone calls help fill in the void, but there are nights when nothing quite seems to compensate for the presence of a warm, loving man sitting on the couch beside her. Dorothy is worried that she is getting older and that she will never meet the right man. She wants to get married again but there are no suitable prospects in sight.

It seems as if Dorothy has spent her whole life worrying about being alone. Even as a teenager, she was concerned about winding up like "Beth the lawyer," her unmarried cousin. Beth was a constant subject of family discussion, sometimes pitied, occasionally admired for her "braininess," but always portrayed as being somehow incomplete. You see, in Dorothy's family, marriage was the most important thing that could happen to a woman, and from the time she started dating, Dorothy viewed every man she met as a possible husband. With every man who tried to kiss her, Dorothy thought, "This could be my chance," and with every man who looked as though he might be backing away, she worried, "I could be losing my last chance; I'll wind up a lonely old maid."

When Dorothy was 22, she met Bob. She knew he wasn't really right for her, but worried that he might be her last good chance. So she decided that she would grow to love him, and when he asked her to marry him, she said yes. They were incredibly bored with each other, but because Dorothy was concerned that she would never meet anyone else, she really tried to hold the marriage together. She failed, and nine rocky years later, the inevitable divorce occurred. Dorothy was hysterical. She couldn't bear to think about spending the rest of her life alone so she started dating with a vengeance. The problem is that instead of being self-protective and discerning, instead of evaluating incompatibilities or areas of conflict, she rationalizes away legitimate concerns and is always ready to tie the knot.

For example, there was Stuart who was a lovely kind man, but they had nothing in common. Nothing! Dorothy listened to the "Oldies but Goodies" stations, he had his ear permanently plugged in on Pavarotti and James Levine; Dorothy was slightly to the left of liberal, he thought Reagan was second only to Nixon; Dorothy believed her psychiatrist was the most important influence in her life, he made fun of therapy and anyone who believed in it. They could never even find a movie or a restaurant that they both enjoyed. Dorothy realized that they might disagree about everything, but she was also worried that it was her last chance. It was a total mismatch. Finally, after two years, one night they started arguing in a restaurant about whether or not the fish was fresh. Within minutes it escalated, and all their differences from wine preferences to their personal feeling about the Iran Contra affair got involved. They both became so out of control, that they were almost arrested. The maître d' suggested that they call it quits. And they did.

Then there was Glen. All he was interested in was sports and the comic pages. He called Dorothy "Babe" and expected her to wash his jock strap and serve him and his friends beer and munchies when they came over to watch tv every weekend. He didn't speak much, but after Stuart, who had an opinion on everything, Dorothy didn't care. She was prepared to spend her life at Madison Square Garden in return for the security of a full-time spouse, but fortunately for everyone, Glen's old girlfriend, the captain of the cheerleaders, called him up one day, and the rest was history.

Finally there was Jason. He was twenty-five years older, and he wanted to move to Arizona to semi-retire. Dorothy thought he was "solid". Besides he didn't argue, and he wasn't interested in sports. Once again, she thought about whether he might also be her last chance, so she actually quit the new job she loved and moved to Arizona to try it out. She felt as though she aged twenty years in twenty-four hours.

Even though Dorothy has now had four last chances, she is still worried about winding up alone and believes more than ever that the next guy who comes along will really be her last chance.

Smart Women Know . . .

Making it on your own is a necessary prerequisite for making it with a partner.

Being married to the wrong man is like being in prison—except you have to make your own meals.

Living with the wrong man can be a thousand times lonelier than living with no man at all.

Smart Women Know . . .
 Sexual Addiction Is A Very Complex
Problem, And You Can't Help Him Solve It.

If you have ever been involved with a man
who is chronically unfaithful, you know how
much it hurts, and how confused and helpless it
makes you feel. When a woman discovers that her
partner is sleeping with someone else, she usually
feels that it is a reflection on her, or on the relationship. What she typically fails to realize is that
a man's sexual behavior may have nothing to do
with her or, for that matter, with any other
woman he may pursue.

Smart Women Know . . .
 Some Men Are *Always* Unfaithful To
Every Woman They Are With.

With these men, it doesn't matter how attractive or desirable a partner may be . . . what ex-
cites them as much as anything else is fulfilling a
fantasy and the thrill of the new experience. It's a

mistake to think that the sex alone is what is exciting them. For some it is the sex combined with the thrill of cheating; for some it is the sex combined with the thrill of a new partner; for some it is the sex combined with the thrill of experimentation. For yet others, it fulfills fantasies of power and control.

Whatever a man's reason may be, as far as a woman is concerned, this kind of behavior is poisonous. It is *his* problem and there is nothing *you* alone can do to bring about the desired change.

Smart Women Know . . .

If You Are Involved With A Man Who Is Chronically Unfaithful, The Smartest Thing You Can Do Is Give Him The Phone Number Of The Nearest Chapter Of Sexaholics Anonymous . . . And Then Walk Away.

Smart Women Know . . .

If He Has Never Been Faithful To Any Other Woman, Don't Expect Him To Be Faithful To You.

Debra is very involved with Timothy. But she is deeply troubled by his history with women, which is marked by a pattern of infidelity and sexual escapades. For example, Timothy's first wife left him because he was having an affair with their next-door neighbor. Timothy has told Debra that his wife knew only half the story—the other half was that he was also sleeping with one of the sopranos in the church choir. Debra met Timothy at work, and even before he confided to her about his sexual past, she had heard far too much office gossip about his behavior with women. Even the district manager's wife was rumoured to be on his list of conquests.

Debra believes that it is different with her and that Timothy's days of infidelity are over. For one thing, he puts down every man he knows who has ever cheated on a partner. For another, Debra doesn't think Timothy would have described his marital behavior as "outrageous" unless he wanted to make it clear that it was a thing of the past. Besides, they have such a torrid sexual relationship that she can't imagine his wanting anyone else. Timothy is the most consistently sexual man Debra has ever met; he is always interested in "going to bed" with her. This is one of the things Debra thinks is special in their relationship.

Although Timothy hasn't said so, Debra is convinced that Timothy was unfaithful to his wife because he wasn't sexually satisfied. She is sure he is sexually satisfied now.

But two weeks ago, Timothy was two hours late meeting her at a party, and he gave her a convoluted explanation. Since then, he seems a little different, and there has been a pattern of unexplained absences. She has confronted him with her fears, but he assures her that her worries are unfounded. Nonetheless, she's beginning to wonder about his behavior. She hates herself for being suspicious and doesn't want to begin steaming open his mail or going through his pockets, but something is giving her a very uncomfortable feeling. Is it possible? Could Timothy be cheating on Debra already?

Smart Women Know . . .

There are two good reasons why you are always the last to know:

- Your partner is always the last to tell.

- You don't really want to know.

The love of a good woman is not enough to change a chronically unfaithful man.

Many men who are chronically unfaithful acknowledge that the best sex they have is the sex they have with their steady partners—but it doesn't matter.

When it comes to sex, some men are completely fantasy driven and, hence, appear insatiable.

Any man who is being led around by his genitals is unsafe to follow.

$\approx$

Some men who are chronically unfaithful are chronically careless about getting caught . . . it's part of the thrill.

$\approx$

Your partner's sexual history is the biggest clue to his sexual future.

$\approx$

Just because a man puts down "guys who sleep around" doesn't mean that he doesn't do it . . . in fact, sometimes it's a sign that he does.

Smart Women Know . . .

There Are Two Times When You Can Get Jealous—When *He* Makes You Jealous And When You Make *Yourself* Jealous; Often Both Are Happening At The Same Time.

Smart Women Know . . .

If you are in a relationship that is making you jealous, it is smart to take a closer look at the relationship—at your partner and at your own reactions.

At one time or another, everyone has experienced jealousy and the accompanying anger, confusion, hurt, and uncertainty. We all know how it makes us feel. What we don't always know, however, is whether or not our jealous feelings are justified. For example:

- You may wonder whether the relationship is such that jealousy is appropriate.

- You may wonder whether your jealousy is all in your head and has no basis in reality.

- You may wonder whether you are creating problems by even considering the possibility of a partner's infidelity.

Here are some questions to ask yourself.

Is your partner truly your partner?
Before you can decide whether or not
your jealousy is appropriate, you have
to determine what kind of
relationship you have. Is fidelity part
of the contract? Or are you involved
with someone who has made it clear
that he is seeing other women.

Smart Women Know . . .
If he isn't monogamous, and you can't
handle it, it's not your jealousy that should
be questioned—it's the whole relationship
and why you are in it.

*Is your partner actively destroying
your relationship contract?*
Monogamy is considered part and
parcel of certain kinds of
relationships. Marriages,
engagements, living together, long-
term relationships, all of these bring
with them the expectation of fidelity.

Smart Women Know . . .

If monogamy is part of your contract, and he's not honoring it, then jealousy is completely justified. However, what is even more appropriate is a reexamination of your relationship, with or without outside help.

Is your jealousy based on feelings you can't confirm?

Sometimes jealousy is based on an intangible "feeling" that can't be defined or confirmed. "But how can I be sure whether he's really seeing someone or whether I'm imagining it?" is the question most women ask. And the only answer is: You can never be 100% sure. However, there are other questions you can ask yourself.

Do you have a history of intense jealousy?

Do you have a history of insecurity in relationships?

Is your jealousy based on fantasies you are spinning in your own mind, or on concrete pieces of information you have obtained?

Do you often find yourself needing more reassurance than any one partner can provide?

If you have a pattern of jealousy, then it is entirely possible that your jealous feelings are the result of your own insecurity. There are, however, some women who are very insecure, who often unwittingly get involved with men who exacerbate these insecurities.

Smart Women Know . . .

Whether he's doing something or you are imagining it, when the relationship is making you respond with jealousy and old self-destructive patterns, then the time has probably come to examine both the relationship and these reactions with the help of a professional.

A Smart Woman Has The Good Sense To
Appreciate A Man Who:
• Has A Full Life Without Her, But Wants To
Be With Her Anyway.
• Listens When *She* Talks To Him.
• Has No Problems With Asking For
Directions If He's Lost.
• Never Orders Her, Or Anybody Else,
Around.
• Doesn't Drive Like Evel Knievel.
• Wants His Spouse To Be An Equal
Partner.
• Is Never A Bully.
• Makes His Loved Ones His First Priority.
• Is More Concerned With What His Kids
Will Think Of Him Than He Is With How
Much He Impresses The Rest Of The World.

Smart Women Know . . .

You have to be extra careful with the man who always plays to win—remember he doesn't always play fair.

Barbara has always been attracted to "power players." Even back in high school, that was the kind of guy who fueled her fantasies. For example, when she was a sophomore in high school, she developed a terrific crush on the guy who was president of the senior class and captain of the debating team. Even after he graduated, she kept a class picture of him hidden away in her locker. Utterly confident about himself, he was voted most likely to succeed. Barbara used to dream that he would become President; she, of course, would be at his side as First Lady. And for a very short time, she thought he would even ask her out, but so many girls were interested in him that she didn't have a chance.

Then when Barbara was twenty-four, she met Stan, a driven young attorney. Stan, who early on in the relationship told Barbara that he was prepared to stake everything for power, glory and success, was also very sure of himself. When they first met, what probably impressed Barbara the most was the way people treated him. He instinctively knew how to get people to do what he wanted. Family, friends, secretaries, associates, headwaiters—everyone was always trying to please him. Some people might describe Stan's behavior as arrogant or controlling, but Barbara found it very sexy . . . at first. By the time they had been married a couple of years, her attitude had totally changed. You see Barbara herself became one of the people who Stan tried to control. He had become completely domineering and the qualities she had originally found attractive had become totally unappealing. She discovered that Stan didn't care about anyone's needs other than his own. He ordered her around, he rarely came home, and Barbara began to suspect some of the late nights involved women as well as work. When she complained, it made the situation even worse. The only time the relationship worked at all was when she did everything he wanted and made no demands whatsoever.

Barbara said that when she told Stan she wanted a divorce, he couldn't believe that she was standing up to him. As always, Stan was determined to have his own way, and the divorce was bitter, ugly, and messy. Barbara came away so exhausted that she wasn't even interested in men for at least a couple of years.

Now Barbara finally feels healed, and she is looking around. She knows what she likes in a man. She likes a man who looks sure of himself, a man who is confident. She likes a man who seems to have power in the world, who gives her a sense that she is being taken care of. But she also remembers that every time she was with a man who wanted to conquer the world, she was the one who ended up feeling defeated.

Smart Women Know . . .

The man who wants to rule the world will probably try to dominate you as well.

When the baby is crying at three a.m., you will be happier with a partner who is there with you instead of one who is in Saudia Arabia clinching a business deal.

With a man who truly craves power, love will always play a weak second.

⚮

Behind many a powerful man sits many a lonely wife.

⚮

A man with an insatiable need for power often has the same appetite for women.

⚮

By the end of the second year of marriage, kindness and consideration count a lot more than a quest for success.

⚮

If you get into a relationship with a man who is known to every headwaiter in town, be prepared to spend a lot of evenings home alone.

Smart Women Know . . .

    After The Breakup Of A Marriage, Or
Any Other Important Relationship, A
Woman Should Expect To Go Through A
Period Of Adjustment Before She Is Ready
To Get Seriously Involved With Another
Man. She Should Be Prepared To Feel:

• As Vulnerable As A Sixteen-Year-Old,
Which Is Why She Needs To Be Very Self-
Protective.

• Still Furious At Her Ex, Which Is Why She
Should Be Careful Not To Transfer Those
Feelings To Other Men.

• Totally Confused As To What Is Expected
Of Her In An Uncommitted Relationship,
Which Is Why She Needs To Beware Of
Compromising Situations.

• Super-Sensitive To Rejection Which Is
Why She May Overreact To Normal Dating
Behavior.

• Unusually Needy And Hungry For
Acceptance, Which Is Why She Can

Respond Too Quickly To Any Man Who Gives Her Assurance And Support In Areas Her Ex May Have Failed Her.

Smart Women Know . . .

After a divorce, it's smart to relearn basic dating skills.

It's been several months since Connie's divorce was finalized and the moment of truth is approaching. After much resistance, Connie's friends have convinced her that she is ready to start dating again. But how do you start dating again when the only interaction you've had with a man for the last twelve years was within the context of a marriage? Connie feels that her marriage was terrible, but nonetheless, her husband was her husband; they had responsibilities for each other, and they had commitment. What will happen when she is with someone to whom she owes nothing, and who owes her nothing in return? It's a clean slate, but what does that mean. Connie is about to find out . . . and she's terrified.

Tomorrow night is Connie's first date with Adam, the cousin of a woman she works with. She's seen him once or twice before when he's visited his cousin, and Connie definitely finds him very attractive. But what if he's as nice as he is good looking? What does a woman do these days on a first date? Is it like you see in the movies with everybody jumping into bed at the first opportunity. And what about birth control? . . . And sexually transmitted diseases? How do you talk about stuff like that, or do you even want to? Sex may be wonderful, but is it worth it? Connie needs some answers *fast.*

Smart Women Know . . .

After a divorce, unless you're careful you can end up in bed with the wrong person—simply because you don't know how to say no without being rejective.

After a divorce, your expectations are apt to be askew so you have to go extra slow.

After a divorce, because you have probably forgotten how nice it feels to be pursued, you are particularly vulnerable to womanizers who are skillful at making a woman feel good about herself—temporarily.

&

Just because you've been married does not mean that you are obligated to have sex with a man on the first date . . . or on any date for that matter. If you feel somehow obligated to show your appreciation to a man who bought you an expensive dinner, send him a Candygram.

Smart Women Know:
• The Threat Of Sexually Transmitted
Diseases Is Affecting Every Single One Of
Us, And We Should All Behave Accordingly.
• Practicing Safe Sex Means A Lot More
Than Carrying A Condom In Your Purse.
• "Natural Skin" Condoms May Feel Better,
But They Don't Offer Sufficient Protection
Against STDs. (Sexually Transmitted
Diseases).
• While A Latex Condom Is The Only Type
That Can Help Prevent STDs, A Condom,
Per Se, Is Not A 100% Guarantee.
• Abstinence Is The Only Complete
Protection Against STDs.
• It Isn't Smart To Carry A Condom And
Not Be Brave Enough To Suggest Using It.
• Oral Sex Is No Protection Against
Sexually Transmitted Disease.
• AIDS Isn't The Only Sexually Transmitted
Disease.
• Nonoxynol-9 Is Not A Pimple Cream; It Is

An Ingredient In Several Over-The-Counter
Contraceptive Creams, And Used Together
With A Condom It May Help Prevent Some
STDs Including AIDS.
• It Is Possible To Contract Any Of The
Sexually Transmitted Diseases From Only
One Incidence Of Intercourse With An
Infected Partner.

Smart Women Know . . .

In The 1990s, A Meaningful Sexual Relationship No Longer Starts With A Kiss; It Starts With A Conversation About Protection Against Sexually Transmitted Diseases.

Anita has had four dates with Tom. Date 1 was lunch. He said "call you soon," and wonder of wonders, he did. Date 2 was the "dinner thing." Afterwards, he said good-night at her door, giving her a quick peck on the cheek. Date 3 was a large party, followed by overtired good-byes and departures in separate taxis (Tom had to catch an early plane the next morning). Date 4 was sort of special because Tom asked Anita to double date with his best friend, and the best friend's wife. Anita felt she must have passed "the test," and afterwards, feeling more comfortable about Tom, she brought him back to her apartment where they necked on the couch until her roommate came home. Tonight Tom is making Anita dinner at his apartment. Tom has no roommates who can walk in at inappropriate moments, and everyone knows what is about to happen . . . Sex. But nobody has discussed the potential dangers of having sexual intercourse in the nineties. Tom looks perfectly safe, and healthy, but Anita is smart enough to know that anyone can get a sexually transmitted disease.

Anita wants to discuss the possible risks both she and Tom face by starting a sexual relationship *before* they start a sexual relationship. In other words, Anita wants to talk about all sexually transmitted diseases, particularly herpes and AIDS. If she is at risk, she wants to know before she gets involved. What should Anita do?

Smart Women Know . . .

It's not smart to be afraid to ask your partner-to-be to provide adequate information about his sexual history.

It's not smart to be afraid to insist upon a monogamous sexual relationship.

~~

Your first responsibility is to protect yourself, and any children you might later have.

~~

If a man is genuinely interested in establishing a serious relationship . . .

. . . he will agree to practice safe sex to make certain that no one risks disease.

. . . he will be prepared to take a blood test.

. . . he will be honest if he has herpes and protect his partner accordingly.

. . . he will agree to stay monogamous for the duration of a relationship.

Smart Women Know . . .

If a man is reluctant to agree to any of these, and you are concerned about STDs, then it's smart to exit the relationship.

Smart Women Know . . .

   The average man is as worried about sexually transmitted diseases as you are.

Anita got up the courage to talk to Tom after dinner on the fifth date. After dinner they were sitting on the couch, hand in hand. Anita knew that there was no way around the issue of sex so she took a deep breath and started a conversation. To her pleasant surprise, Tom welcomed the discussion. He told her that he had not had a sexual relationship for almost a year, which was about as long as it had been for Anita. They both agreed that they liked each other and wanted to have a sexual relationship with each other. Although to the best of their knowledge, neither Tom nor Anita had been involved with anyone from any of the known high risk groups, they felt that blood tests were a good idea, for both of them, and they agreed to practice safe sex until they were comfortable with the results of those tests. Anita was very happy that she had the conversation. It may have decreased the romance, but it increased the sense of intimacy and trust between her and Tom.

Smart Women Know . . .
   There Is Nothing Wrong And Everything Right In Having A Serious Discussion About The Dangers Of Sexually Transmitted Diseases With Any Potential Partner.

Smart Women Know . . .
    The Only Time You Should Believe The
Man Who Says "I'll Pull Out" Is When You're
Waiting For His Parking Space.

Smart Women Know . . .
    Getting Pregnant Is Not The Perfect
Way To Start A New Relationship.

Tom and Anita are about to celebrate the results of their blood tests. Everyone can breathe a little easier, and Tom is looking forward to tossing the rest of those condoms into the fireplace.

But Anita is not so eager to fuel Tom's bonfire, because they still haven't discussed how they will handle birth control from here on forward. Anita doesn't want to put out Tom's fire by more heavy discussions, but Anita is very clear about the fact that she doesn't want to get pregnant. What should she do? What should she know? What should she say?

A Smart Woman Knows there are only two times she can get pregnant—when she wants to . . . and when she doesn't want to.

A Smart Woman also Knows that she is the only one she can really trust to protect her body.

❧

A Smart Woman Knows that it is better to appear "ready" than to deal with the consequences of an unplanned pregnancy.

❧

A Smart Woman Knows that most men are as uncomfortable as women are when it comes to discussing the issue of birth control.

❧

A Smart Woman Knows that men think that a woman is in charge of birth control because "It's her body."

❧

A Smart Woman Knows that the typical man doesn't raise the birth control issue because he thinks that if the woman doesn't say something she is taking care of it (i.e., she is on the pill, using an IUD, or wearing a diaphragm).

❧

A Smart Woman Knows that if she doesn't have a form of birth control, it's up to her to say something.

A Smart Woman is smart enough to discuss
birth control while her clothes are still on.

Smart Women Know That In A Good Relationship:

• Both Partners Are Supportive Of Each Other's Needs And Goals.

• Neither Partner Tries To Change Or Control The Other.

• Both Partners Are Accepting Of Each Other's Limitations.

• Neither Partners Insist Upon Unconditional Love.

• Both Partners Respect The Other's Boundaries.

• Neither Partner Resents The Other's Individuality.

• Both Partners Have An Equal Voice.

• Both Partners Are Genuinely And Equally Committed.

Smart Women Know . . .

An insecure and abusive man finds it easier to knock you down to his level rather than to raise himself up to yours.

Karen started going out with Ed because he seemed genuinely interested in her. Now she has been with him for a little over six months, and she's getting scared. He's changed—drastically. When she first met him, he was so gentle with her, so kind, so attentive. That's what she liked about him; that and the fact that he was single-minded in his efforts to get Karen to make a commitment to him. She liked being wanted that much; it made her feel secure.

Ed's biggest drawback was probably his insecurity. Karen figured that Ed's parents must have done something wrong because he was so unsure of himself in so many areas. Karen decided without telling him that it was her job to help him feel more secure . . . more certain of himself.

But once they moved in together, everything was different. He began to criticize her, small things at first, like the way she cooked eggs and the way she made the bed. At first she didn't argue with him because she thought once he was more secure with her, it would all get better. Now it seems as though he lives for the chance to put her down. He tells her that he knows what's best for her, and he finds fault with everything. The way she dresses. The way she eats. What she eats.

And instead of becoming more secure, he has become almost paranoid. Anything and everything makes him jealous. At first Karen thought it was because he loved her so much—now she feels that it's sick. She has to give him a minute by minute accounting of her time when she is out of the house. He's screening her phone calls. He was always slightly controlling sexually, now he is becoming practically unbearable. Sometimes he screams at her for no reason. He tells her that she doesn't pay attention to him when he's talking. He's totally unreasonable; for example, he never does anything to help her, but he criticizes the way she cleans house.

Lots of times after he's been particularly difficult, he seems to be genuinely sorry for the way he acts. Then he apologizes. Karen is beginning to feel that her life is being governed by his moods. It's so upsetting when he gets angry, and she finds herself embarassed by the way she listens to him.

As time goes on, she can feel herself becoming more and more dependent on him . . . but she's also beginning to hate him. She doesn't understand it. She doesn't know what to do. She worries that things could get out of control. When she fights back, he gets so angry that she is afraid he will hit her.

Karen isn't sure whether or not she would define Ed as abusive.

Smart Women Know . . .

Whether it's emotional or physical, abuse is abuse.

If a man puts you down, he is trying to lower your self-esteem so that you will be more dependent on him.

Abusive behavior frequently reveals itself in stages with emotional abuse preceding physical abuse; *no* form of abuse is acceptable.

Smart Women Know . . .

    If A Man Seems Obsessed With Trying To Control You And Your Behavior, He Is Being Emotionally Abusive.

There is a difference between being helpful and supportive and being controlling. If he is being helpful and supportive, he is doing it for your benefit, if he is being controlling, he is doing it for his. A smart woman knows that there are a variety of ways in which a controlling man can try to manipulate your behavior.

- He can control with money.

- He can control by sabotaging your
      work or other interests.

- He can control by trying to crush
      your ego (finding fault, putting
      you down, belittling your
      accomplishments).

- He can control by trying to isolate or alienate you from friends and family.

- He can control you with unending demands.

- He can control by using threats (of infidelity or of leaving, for example).

- He can control with his moods.

- He can control with his inaccessibility.

- He can control with his temper.

Smart Women Know . . .

The abusive man is not a myth; any woman can meet one, and they can be found in all age groups and at all socio-economic levels.

Donna is recovering from a relationship with an insanely jealous man. From the day they moved in together, he was emotionally abusive and eventually he began hitting her whenever he had too much to drink. At first she associated this behavior solely with liquor or drug use. But she has spoken to other women who have been involved with abusive men who were not substance abusers. Donna would like some guidelines to help warn her away from a man who might become abusive. She wants to know early in the relationship, before she gets involved with someone, if the potential for abuse exists.

Smart Women Know . . .

It's smart to recognize the warning signs of a potential abuser. The more you see, the greater your risk. And the more self-protective you need to be about getting involved.

- Does he have any problems with drinking or drugs?

- Does he have a history of work-related problems?

- Is he without good friends, men and women who have known him for a long time?

- Do you get the feeling that he is someone who needs you to save him?

- Is he extremely possessive?

- Is he pushing you to make a commitment before an appropriate amount of time has passed?

- Does he show any signs of unprovoked jealousy?

- Does he try to isolate you from your friends and family?

- Does he have a serious problem with self-esteem?

- Is he disassociated from his social environment (no real roots)?

- Does he make you feel that you are the only one who can understand him or really care about him?

- Does he show signs of a bad temper or a low frustration tolerance?

Smart Women Know . . .
 It's Never Smart To Bend Yourself
Into A Pretzel Trying To Accommodate A
Man.

When a woman makes herself completely available to a man, changing her schedule to accomodate his, changing her needs to accomodate his, changing her priorities to accomodate his, she typically justifies it by saying that no one is forcing her to do this—that it is totally by choice and what she wants to do. Nonetheless, a smart woman knows that this is not a smart way to behave.

So many women have made the mistake of altering their lives so that all their choices will reflect what they perceive to be male needs. But few men, contemporary and otherwise, truly appreciate this behavior. Most of them ultimately tend to view it as a statement of expectation, or a demand to behave accordingly. Some are immediately turned off; others are willing to take advantage of it temporarily.

Smart Women Know . . .
      Dependency Is A Turn Off, Not A Turn On.

Smart Women Know . . .

A relationship with a man should enrich your life, not define it.

Bonnie acknowledges that she has difficulty establishing relationships that work. You see, although most people think of Bonnie as self-sufficient, competent, and independent, when she meets a man she likes, she gets too caught up in being with him. Almost against her will, she finds herself becoming clingy, needy, and insecure. In short, she becomes overly involved and dependent.

If a man doesn't call every day, she becomes anxious—even at the beginning of a relationship. If she doesn't know for sure when she will see him again, she gets nervous. For example, when she returns home from an evening with someone she likes, Bonnie will often find herself reaching for the phone to call him. She can't bear the anxiety of wondering when she will see him again, or if she will see him again. Before she even knows if she likes him, she begins thinking about all the little things she wants to share with him—like every aspect of her life. She is prepared to give up her friends, her plans, her entire lifestyle almost as soon as she meets someone. It sounds silly but she is afraid to make other plans in case "he" calls and wants to do something. She worries that if she's not available to him, she may lose the opportunity to "have him." In short, she is willing to rearrange her life.

For example, she has only recently started dating Daniel, a lawyer she met a couple of months ago. At first the relationship was very even. Daniel was obviously interested in her, and after a few phone calls, they went out to dinner. So far, so good. Bonnie felt calm and in control of herself and her feelings. Then after their fourth date, they started to neck, one thing led to another, and they wound up almost having sex. This is the point at which Bonnie always starts getting anxious. Once a physical contact has been established, she needs a great deal of reassurance, she begins dreaming about the future, she starts fantasizing about the kind of the life "the two of them" will have, and she starts trying to push the relationship to a new plateau of intimacy.

Daniel is very engrossed in his career, and establishing a permanent relationship isn't his first priority. Nonetheless they both like each other, and there is plenty of room for the relationship to grow. Bonnie, who senses that Daniel isn't thrilled by needy women, realizes that he is doing what's right for him. So she's doing everything she can to control her behavior. For example, instead of phoning Daniel when she needs reassurance, she's calling her friends.

When Bonnie's last two relationships broke up, she wasn't sure whether or not she had precipitated the break-up by her demands. Bonnie doesn't want it to happen again, but she really isn't sure about what to do. She doesn't mean to be demanding; she thinks that waiting for a man to validate her is the same thing as being feminine.

Smart Women Know . . .

Men respect women who retain their boundaries.

The best way to develop a good relationship is to maintain the relationship you have already developed with yourself.

A desirable woman doesn't rearrange her priorities every time she meets a prospective partner.

A man who is interested in you is not going to disappear simply because you are busy.

It's not smart to fantasize about "a life" with someone you hardly know.

The stronger and more independent you are, the better your relationships will be.

Clinging is not a synonym for feminine.

Smart Women Know . . .

It's Not Smart To Set Up A Pattern In
A Relationship In Which "He" Becomes The
Sultan, And You Become The Grape Peeler.

Like it or not, we are still all conditioned by the
stereotypes of the fifties. How could it be otherwise? Walk past any newsstand, and you will see
whole magazines that are devoted to such wifely
skills as cooking, entertaining, balancing budgets,
and decorating. Not that there is anything wrong
with these things in the right place at the right
time. But the beginning of a relationship is neither the right place nor the right time.

If you trot out all your wifely skills at the
beginning of a relationship, the average man
doesn't quite know what to do. The facts: He has
seen the same magazines you have; he knows
what a home cooked meal in a romantic setting is
supposed to do. Therefore, he immediately as-
sumes you are either trying to get him to marry
you or you are trying to get him into bed. How
does that make him feel? Sometimes it can make

a man feel as though he is the child and you are the mommy; other times he feels as though he is playing a fifties dating game or acting out a tired Playboy fantasy. More often than not, it makes him feel uncomfortable. Remember that "playing house" has never been a game that men understand. End result: Instead of appreciating how wonderful you are, he may think that you are trying too hard because there is something wrong with you.

A Smart Woman Knows:
• You Don't Have To Prove Yourself Worthy.
• You Don't Have To Prove That You're Smart.
• You Don't Have To Prove That You're A Good Person.
• You Don't Have To Prove That You're A Terrific Cook.
• You Don't Have To Prove That You're Funny.
• You Don't Have To Prove That You Are Sympathetic.

• You Don't Have To Prove That You Are Supportive.
Etc., Etc., Etc.

Smart Women Know . . .

If you really love to cook, cook for your friends—not for your dates.

Diana wants Ted to like her. They've been out a few times, and once he told her that he was tired of eating all his meals out of plastic containers. After consulting with a couple of friends, she has invited him to dinner, thinking a home-cooked meal might blaze a path to his heart. The last issue of her favorite women's magazine had all the ingredients for a truly romantic supper for two, so she's following their advice, and some of their menu: Candles, wine, poached salmon, lemon souffle, the whole bit.

The night before the "big dinner," she spends several tedious hours cleaning her apartment—waxing, polishing, buffing, scrubbing. When she is finished, it sparkles. On the day of the big dinner, Diana races out of her office at 12:30 and runs home, stopping at the greengrocer and fish market on the way (everything has to be fresh, of course). In her apartment, she puts everything away, and sets the table before heading back to the office and an emergency meeting. At 5:45, she rushes out arriving home at 6:15, just in time to give the place one last straightening, trim the wicks, make the salad dressing, wash the arugula, arrange the flowers. At 6:45, right on schedule she hurtles into the shower. And by 7:05 when the doorbell rings, the salad greens are washed and tossed, the salmon is waiting, and the souffle is rising on schedule. Diane looks elegant and lovely. She feels like a wreck.

Diane may be efficient, but is she being smart? Will her efforts have the effect she desires?

Smart Women Know . . .

If a man really likes you, it will be months before he notices whether or not you can boil water.

If he falls in love with you, it's going to be for who you are, not what you can broil.

A home-cooked meal, no matter how perfectly prepared, is no longer the best way to a man's heart.

"House" is a game you can play with your husband, not with a date.

Attempts to make yourself look like you have "perfect wife potential" often garner the opposite reaction.

A pull-out-all-the-stops dinner at the beginning of a relationship frequently makes it seem as though you're "trying too hard."

It isn't smart to exhaust yourself to impress a man, and it isn't necessary.

Some men are put off by wifely skills.

Many men react to a home-cooked meal as if it is the bait in a husband trap; there is a fine line between impressing a man and scaring him to death.

A Smart Woman Knows When To Cut Her Losses.

The relationship has been going on for more than two years, and nothing is changing. He is the same man you fell madly in love with, but he is no closer to becoming the kind of man who can give you what you want. A lot of push me/pull me has gone on between the two of you—as well as many mixed messages. There are moments when the relationship seems almost idyllic—but all too often, it feels like hell. Despite all the hard times, you still love him to pieces. In fact it seems, sometimes, as though the two of you have been through so much together, you have a stronger bond that the average couple celebrating their golden wedding anniversary. Nonetheless, no matter what you do, what you say, what you feel, the relationship is going nowhere.

It's heartbreaking and it's sad, but when you think about it realistically—think about who he is and how he is—you can see that your dreams of a future with him are not going to materialize.

152

Smart Women Know . . .
    It's Painful To Let Go Of A Dream, But
Sometimes It's The Only Smart Thing To
Do.

Smart Women Know . . .

Waiting for a man to change is like waiting to be told that you've won the Publisher's Clearing House Sweepstakes.

Laura is madly in love with Phil. She has been for years. She believes that he is also in love with her. She bases this belief on the fact that he keeps coming back to her. He is also deeply passionate, and the sex is terrific. In fact, everything about the relationship is intense. From the very beginning it has been a roller coaster ride. She sees the connection between the two of them as being karmic, and she can't imagine being with anyone else. After all, they have been through so much together.

Laura spends most of her time thinking about Phil. In addition she spends a great deal of time talking about Phil, mostly to her best friend, Patti, and anyone else who will listen. She also spends an inordinate amount of time waiting for Phil to call and waiting for Phil to show up. In the course of the relationship, Laura has had a lot to talk about. Sometimes Phil stops calling altogether. When this happens, Laura becomes a basket case. Phil has started at least three relationships with other women—that she knows of. Once she vowed never to see him again. But when he started calling again, she relented. In some of their more intimate moments, Phil has acknowledged that he is immature. He tells Laura that he doesn't know why she puts up with him.

You see, Laura is waiting for Phil to change, to grow up, and to realize how important she is to him. In short she is waiting for a miracle. In the meantime, she tries to be understanding and loving. She worries about setting an example for him so she doesn't do anything that could be regarded as retaliatory. In other words, she is totally faithful, totally committed.

The only friend who is willing to listen to Laura is Patti. They talk on the phone together, each hoping that call-waiting will interrupt them with a call from "him." Patti is also waiting—in her case it is for the man she loves to leave his wife. Patti and Laura have a great deal in common. They are both frequently alone; they are both unhappy much of the time; they have both put their lives on "hold."

Smart Women Know . . .

Some relationships just weren't meant to be.

In Hollywood movies, men "come to their senses" and rush after the "good woman" who has loved them through it all; in the real world, it doesn't seem to work that way.

Some men do change, but when they do, they often change women as well.

It's smart to be secure enough to leave a man whose choices are making you emotionally insecure.

If a man tells you he doesn't know why you put up with him, he knows what he's talking about.

Unless he works for the Post Office, there is no reason why any man should need more than a few weeks "to sort things out."

Smart Women Know . . .
   It's Always Smart To Find Out As
Much As Possible About A Man *Before* You
Get Involved With Him, Not After.

Nothing can tell you more about what you can expect from a man than a thorough examination of his personal history. If he doesn't make this information available to you, take it as a warning because a sincere man should have a sincere history that includes:

• one or more real interests

• a verifiable work history that reflects
   his education and background

• no serious unresolved problems such
   as substance abuse

• no ongoing serious relationships with
   other women

- a real group of friends, some of whom he has known for a long period of time

- a real family to whom he still speaks

- past relationships that aren't all shrouded in secrecy

- at least one ex-girlfriend with whom he is still friendly

- at least one period of time when he has been without a relationship, a time when he has been concentrating on other things

Smart Women Know . . .

If You Are Trying To Turn Your Life Into A Soap Opera, It's Time To Change The Channel.

They have been dating three months. They have shared all and bared all—their histories, their mysteries; their public lives, their private parts. Now it's time to get back to the real world. One of them wants to read a book and watch David Letterman. The other one gets nervous and starts wondering, "Is this all there is?" This isn't the way it is in the movies. How do I know that the one I love really loves me? Where are the flames?

Smart Women Know . . .

If You Want Flames Every Night, Join The Fire Department.

Smart Women Know . . .

Sturm und Drang make for a good evening at the theatre, but not for a good relationship.

Allison's life seems more like a mini-series than a real life. And even Allison is beginning to see why. It seems that she is so uncomfortable with an even, easy relationship . . . so distrusting that it can last . . . that she finds herself constantly creating crises to bring her and Jim closer together. Or sometimes, at least temporarily, to pull them apart. She realized what she was doing one night when she and Jim were out for dinner. For a few minutes everything in the relationship was fine—but she felt as though there was nothing going on, nothing to talk about, nothing with a high enough level of intensity. It seems as though when things start getting calm, Allison immediately starts missing the excitement of a new relationship.

Allison can't remember the last time her relationship with Jim felt settled for more than five minutes. Perhaps it was right before she decided to take her first vacation alone. Or was it right before her first depression? Maybe it was right before the night she talked so much about her "successful and sexy" new lawyer that Jim walked out in a jealous rage. When the relationship gets calm, Allison gets a little scared—the question, "Is this all there is?" keeps playing over and over in her head. If a man isn't fighting with her . . . if she isn't getting emotional feedback, she questions what is going on. And when she and the man in her life aren't arguing, she worries that it might be too even; she worries that the man might be getting bored. What this means is that she is always revving things up. When she goes out with a man, she never wants to discuss the movie they just saw—she always wants to talk about their "feelings" for each other, and what those feelings mean.

Allison doesn't like to think of herself as someone who sabotages relationships but her therapist and friends are all beginning to wonder. Remember how she practically drove Mark into the arms of another woman by being so possessive that she never let him out of her sight? And Roger . . . how caring he was until Allison started feeling smothered by Roger's good intentions? She asked him for space and he complied

. . . he moved to Arizona and was married to another woman within the year. Of course there was Felix . . . but Felix came with his own collection of built-in crises, including a wife and an emotionally disturbed child. It's true Felix was always "feeling" something, but other relationships consumed most of his emotional intensity.

Allison says she longs for a committed relationship. But her actions speak very differently. Even she is beginning to wonder if she'll ever be able to have a comfortable, stable relationship. She used to think her problem was that she chose the wrong men, but now she's not so certain. She is beginning to wonder if it is the way she behaves.

Smart Women Know . . .

Many therapists say that women who sabotage their relationships have deep-rooted fears of rejection—these often compel her to turn the situation into a self-fulfilling prophecy.

Creating perpetual crises will ultimately drive any healthy man away; only the twisted linger.

It's smart to learn to accept and enjoy the quiet periods in your relationships.

Smart Women Know That It's Smart To
Think Twice And Ask Many Questions
Before Continuing A Relationship With . . .
       . . . Any Man Who Gets Less
Interested In You As You Get More
Interested In Him.

or

. . . Any Man Who Gets More Interested In
You As You Get Less Interested In Him.

Smart Women Know The Difference
Between . . .

. . . being manipulative and being self-
protective.

Barbara Jean is having a great deal of trouble
with her boyfriend, Sam. As far as Sam is concerned, Barbara Jean is made of putty and mush.
No matter what he does or doesn't do, she continues to behave as though he is the world's most
precious person. Her friends, who are tired of
watching her turn herself into a total doormat for
someone who doesn't appreciate her, suggest that
she force herself to behave differently. That way
maybe she will force Sam to change. Here are
some of the things they have suggested that she
try:

- Barbara Jean should play hard to get
  and act as though she's not
  interested in Sam.

- Barbara Jean should try to make
  Sam jealous by telling him that

she is going out with someone
else.

- Barbara Jean should play "phone
  games"—take the receiver off the
  hook, screen her calls, make him
  think that she's never home,
  don't call him back right away,
  have a man answer her phone,
  always be the first one to hang
  up.

- Barbara Jean should change her
  behavior and become moody and
  unpredictable.

- Barbara Jean should reject every
  third date.

- Barbara Jean should act sexually
  dissatisfied or mention some other
  man's name during sex.

- Barbara Jean should make up some
  "story" to get his attention.

- Barbara Jean should etc., etc.

Other friends tell Barbara Jean that manipulation doesn't work in the long run. They tell Barbara Jean that she can't continue manipulating

Sam for the rest of her life. They suggest that she try an honest approach. Barbara Jean says that she has been honest about her feelings, and that it hasn't worked.

Because Barbara Jean is mostly worried about "losing" Sam, she is is afraid. She thinks that if she "plays hard to get" Sam may go out and get somebody else. Besides, she says she doesn't want to be manipulative and it doesn't feel right pretending to be someone other than herself. What should she do?

Smart women know that game playing may work to change a relationship, but any change will only be temporary. Barbara Jean needs to start making some *real* changes in how she feels. By definition that will change the relationship. In short, Barbara Jean needs to stop worrying about how to change Sam's behavior. Instead she needs to start thinking about how to change her attitude so that eventually she no longer cares what Sam does or doesn't do. You see, being self-protective and taking care of yourself is not game playing. It's a real statement, and it will produce real results.

Smart Women Know The Difference
Between . . .

   . . . playing hard to get and *being* hard
to get.

   . . . *acting* as though you're not that
interested in him and *actively* pursuing your
own interests.

Smart Women Know . . .

It's Not Smart To Hang On To The Pain.

When a relationship with someone you love has ended, there is a strong tendency to keep going over the details: every dinner you shared, every movie you watched, every conversation, every nuance, everything *he* said, everything *you* said. You worry whether you did something wrong, whether you did everything you could. You become annoyed with yourself because you don't remember everything—perhaps the crucial event that ended the relationship occurred while you weren't paying attention. This kind of thinking happens to just about everyone. It's very human, but it isn't going to help you get over the pain. It's human to think about how you could have changed the outcome, and it's human to wonder if there is anything you can say or do that will patch things up, but this kind of thinking doesn't help you take care of you . . . and taking care of *you* is your first and foremost responsibility.

A Smart Woman Knows . . .

If "He" Caused The Breakup, It's Up To Him To Put It Back Together. You Have To Get On With Your Own Life.

Smart Women Know . . .

This is an absolute fact! Once you get over the pain of the breakup—*and you will* —you will wonder what on earth you saw in him in the first place.

It's been almost three months since Peter told Lisa that he didn't see any future in their relationship. Three long, painful months. Some days it hurt so much, Lisa didn't know what to do with herself. Peter was the man with whom she had hoped to spend the rest of her life. As far as Lisa was concerned, the only problem in the relationship was that they weren't already engaged. She certainly didn't expect it to end. In fact, from where Lisa stood, the relationship appeared to be growing stronger, and heading for a commitment. The split hit her like a crosstown bus. And the fact that it happened the week before Christmas magnified everything a hundredfold.

For weeks Lisa has been just dazed . . . shocked by the pain. Putting one foot in front of the other to get through each day is an effort . . .

barely eating . . . alternating between not being able to sleep and wanting to crawl into her bed and shut out the world. She is convinced that she'll never meet another man like Peter . . . that she'll never love another man the way she loved Peter.

Lisa realizes that she has to get better and get over this, but she is crushed. Oftentimes she becomes enraged at Peter for causing the breakup. They were best friends, lovers . . . how could he have betrayed her like this? Why is he not bothered by it? Doesn't he miss her? Other times Lisa stops trying to understand Peter's behavior and wonders what she did wrong. She thinks about the things she said, the things she did. If she had behaved differently, maybe the relationship would have turned out differently. Most of the time, Lisa just wants Peter back. Although she knows his behavior was unacceptable, she is all too ready to take him back . . . if he asks. But he hasn't asked.

Lisa's friends tell her she should start dating other men. They insist it will make her feel better. They tell her to take a vacation by herself somewhere far away from places that will remind her of the time she spent with Peter. They tell her to get more involved in her work . . . that no man is worth this much suffering . . . that Peter was a creep. Intellectually, Lisa understands the advice her friends are giving her. It is advice she has often given to them under similar circumstances. But it all seems so wrong. She doesn't want to meet another man . . . she wants Peter. There is no place to go that won't remind her of Peter. And as far as her work is concerned, she can barely concentrate . . . how can she bury herself in it?

She has so many contradictory feelings that she is completely confused. One part of her only wants Peter to explain what happened. Another part wants a chance to prove to him that no other woman can make him happy. Another part wants a chance to get even. She feels as though there is nobody but Peter who could understand the intensity of her feelings, but he's the one person she can't talk to.

Some days Lisa feels a little better, but then just when she starts to notice whether or not the sun is shining, something will happen and she'll be right back where she started, lonely and depressed. How long does this take, anyway?

Smart Women Know . . .

Although grieving the loss of a relationship takes time, the idea is to get out of pain as quickly as possible—that means not looking back.

Trying to be friends with a man who just broke your heart is about as self-protective as taking up sky diving.

Dating after a breakup is a dangerous game. If you have even one bad blind date, you may become convinced that you will never again meet anyone you like and that "he" was the only man for you. And if you meet someone else you like even a little bit, your needs may propel you into getting involved too quickly.

Trying to get "him" to give you a reasonable explanation for the breakup is a waste of time . . . you'll never be satisfied with what he says.

Your feelings are always magnified and distorted after a breakup and you should never act quickly or impulsively on these feelings.

❧

Breakups always seem to happen at the worst possible time; they tend to occur right smack in the middle of a holiday or a family crisis: the week before Christmas, the day before the Fourth of July, Valentines Day, and your birthday are the norm.

❧

Begging, pleading, crying, and letter writing will usually only push the person initiating the breakup further away. If you have to write, mail the letter to yourself. When you need to cry, cry to your friends.

❧

The kind of relationship you want back is often the kind of relationship you never had in the first place.

❧

Although you may not believe it, you will survive the breakup, and emerge stronger and wiser.

❧

The man who splits up with you tends to come back into your life the moment you decide you don't want him anymore.

Image:

"Wanting him back" is probably not what you really want . . . it's just what you want when you're hurting.

Image:

Getting over the loss of a love seems to take forever, and there is a lot of back and forthing. It's important for you to know, and believe, that you will get over this; just keep taking care of yourself.

Image:

Sometimes the best way to take care of yourself is to find competent, sympathetic, professional counseling.

Smart Women Know That After The Breakup, You Should *Not* Think About . . .

- how *he* is feeling right now.

- what *he* is doing right now.

- other women he may have met.

- how much he is going to miss you.

- what you might have done to prevent the breakup.

- what you might have said to prevent the breakup.

- what you will miss most about him.

- your intimate times together.

- how you can get him back.

- how you can get revenge.

Smart Women Know That After The Breakup, You *Should* Think About . . .

- a vacation.

- all the positive qualities you may find in the new men you're going to meet—qualities "he" didn't have.

- your freedom.

- the most sleazy or stupid thing he ever did.

- wonderful things about yourself that he never appreciated.

- all the things you've sacrificed for this relationship (places you wanted to go, things you wanted to do . . . that he wasn't interested in).

- all his bad qualities (too boring, too demanding, too needy, too whiney, too controlling, too insensitive, too cheap, too self-absorbed, etc.)

- the people in your life who are always there for you.

- all the time you'll have to do things with your friends again.

- a present you deserve just for being you.

Smart Women Know . . .

If He Doesn't Make You Feel Good About Yourself, Then He's Not Good For You.

Talk to any group of women who are happy in their relationships, and you will discover a common denominator: They are with men whose words and behavior encourage their partners to feel intelligent, attractive, and generally terrific. Men who like women convey this by making their partners feel secure.

Smart Women Know . . .

Some men pit women against each other; these men should be avoided.

Fred has a history of being involved with two women at once. He's usually getting out of one relationship and into another. And when he's in the new relationship, he doesn't stop looking. There are periods when he isn't actually involved with someone, but even then, he has more "platonic" women friends than seems humanly possible. In fact, if you were to discuss Fred with one of these "platonic" friends, she would probably tell you that she doesn't think it's totally platonic, that he is totally seductive emotionally, and that he flirts like crazy.

There are other periods in Fred's life when he is actively involved with two or more women at the same time; then he is in "terrible conflict" and can't decide what to do. It makes all the women feel terrible. Typically a woman starts trying to do more to please Fred; she starts trying to prove herself. She is always convinced that

Fred would be wisest to be with her. Sometimes she gets so upset and so jealous that she enters therapy or joins a support group. Then she is apt to spend most of her time discussing Fred's "problem."

Mona is Fred's ex-wife. Better than anyone else, she knows all the ways in which Fred can set up situations in which women find themselves in competition. She would tell you that it wasn't only the women Fred had affairs with, it was everyone. When they were first married, Fred subtly encouraged small disagreements between Mona and her mother-in-law. Mona sometimes also found herself caught up in odd conflicts with her sister-in-law. And then there were the women Fred worked with. What exactly did he do that always made Mona regard them as direct competition?

When Fred talks about women, he frequently sounds like a judge in an offbeat beauty pageant: "She's very pretty . . . . She's smart . . . . She's talented . . . . She makes a great pot roast . . . . She has flabby thighs . . . . She isn't aging well." When a woman is with Fred, she is usually not consciously aware of what he is doing. All she knows is that she is feeling defensive and that somehow she wants to do something to prove that she is worthy.

Smart Women Know . . .

A man who hates women sometimes has a way of making women hate each other.

If a man is making you feel as though you have to "be the best" to get his attention or his approval, he has a problem with women that you can't solve.

Men who regard all women as contenders for their affection are not capable of real intimacy.

Men who have a compare-and-contrast attitude towards relationships are not just picky, they're narcissistic.

Any man who has two women fighting over him probably doesn't deserve either one of them.

Smart Women Know That In A Good Marriage:
• Both Partners Have Room To Grow.
• Self Esteem Is Reinforced, Not Threatened.
• Both Partners Have Equal Rights.
• Sex Isn't Always Perfect, But It Doesn't Matter.
• Independence Is Encouraged.
• Separate Interests Are Not Threatening.
• Chores Are Shared.
• Differences Are Negotiated.
• There Is Room For Honest Give And Take.
• Nobody Hogs The Hot Water.

Smart Women Know . . .

Every long-term relationship has a list of situations that need negotiating.

Anna and Gary have been married and living together for almost a year now. At first, everything was perfect. They always wanted to watch the same tv shows, eat at the same restaurants, visit the same friends, sleep the same hours. But, like all relationships, it was just a matter of time before this "pink period" began to wind down.

At this point, both Anna and Gary are first finding out that they are not attached at the hip. Gary is beginning to dissent on the restaurant choices. Anna is getting tired of watching "his tv shows"—some nights she would prefer only her favorites. Gary puts the news on the minute he walks through the door—it's getting on Anna's nerves. Anna's work load has increased and she finds herself drifting off to sleep by ten p.m. Gary can never go to sleep without reading in bed, even though the light usually makes it difficult for Anna to sleep very well. Anna would like her dog,

Elvis, to be able to spend the night at the foot of their bed. Gary insists that a dog's place is on the floor. Anna's cat, Rosebud, is determined to share Gary's pillow. Anna wonders if Rosebud loves Gary best—Gary wonders if he should see a good allergist. These kinds of conflicts seems to be appearing more frequently. Gary and Anna are able to discuss their differences, but neither is ever totally content with compromise. What happened to "the two hearts that beat as one"?

They both recognize that they are becoming less patient and more easily angered. Something has to give, otherwise there may be some major fighting not far down the road. But they wonder if everyone has to do this. And they wonder if it's worth it. And neither of them can believe that they are quibbling over the same kind of "who squeezed the toothpaste in the middle" stuff that their parents did.

Smart Women Know . . .

The only person you are totally compatible with is yourself.

No matter how much you love each other, if you are human and have personalities, you are not going to agree about everything—differences are a part of life, not immediate grounds for a breakup.

Conflicts have to be discussed and negotiated, and both partners have to be prepared to compromise.

People who can't share territory may be better off living alone.

A Smart Woman Knows How To Give Love
Without Giving Up A Part Of Herself.

Smart Women Know . . .

It's smart to be who you are and to be the best you can be.

When Lana plays chess with her boyfriend, Stanley, she always lets him win. She's a good enough chess player so that she can throw a game without it looking obvious.

Marilyn and her husband, Dan, are lawyers in the same office. Marilyn expends a great deal of energy making certain that Dan looks as though he is a more effective lawyer than she is. She figures that once he gets to be partner, she can start worrying about doing more for her own career.

Diana and her fiancé, Tom, are renovating their house. When Diana was living alone, she single-handedly rebuilt her apartment. She is a whiz with sheetrock and plaster. However she is standing aside looking helpless while Tom wildly waves an electric drill. She doesn't want to show

Tom what to do because she doesn't think it's "feminine."

৵৹

Lorraine and her husband, Frank, disagree vehemently about some political candidates. Lorraine knows that Frank loves to debate political issues with his friends. Nonetheless, she is nervous about articulating some of her well thought-out opinions when they are talking with friends. Instead she keeps quiet and lets Frank do all the talking.

Lana, Marilyn, Diana, and Lorraine have something in common. They believe the "big lie" and deny large chunks of themselves because they think "that's what you have to do to have a man in your life." Unfortunately, they are not unique. Most of us have received very specific and very slanted advice and information about how even the most liberated woman should behave when she is with a man. This advice reflects an underlying theme. It says: If a woman wants a relationship, she had better be good at pretending.

What do smart women know about advice that tells a woman to be less—or different—than she really is? Smart women know that much of the folklore about what makes a relationship function focuses on *his* needs, not hers. This advice is not always smart. For example:

> *"You have to flatter a man's ego. Men have very fragile egos."*
>
> Smart Women Know: Most of us—male and female—have fragile egos. If taking care of his ego obliterates yours, you're not protecting yourself, and you're not being very smart.

> *"A man should always make more money than the woman. After all, men are the natural hunters."*
>
> Smart Women Know: If purposely suppressing your earning capacity—or concealing your earning capacity—is a necessary ingredient in his happiness, then the relationship is not going to allow you to grow or fulfill your potential.

> *"A man doesn't like it when a woman seems smarter than he is."*
>
> Smart Women Know: If a man is threatened by a woman's intelligence, then *he* isn't smart enough to appreciate what makes *you* special.

❦

*"The man should be the one to
initiate sex."*

> Smart Women Know: A secure man
> isn't disturbed by a woman who is
> confident enough to express her
> sexual needs.

❦

*"The man of the house is supposed to
be in charge of things! He should
have the final say."*

> Smart Women Know: Like any other
> partnership, a relationship works best
> if it is founded on a 50/50 basis;
> when it comes to decision making
> that means both partners are equal.

❦

"Men don't like opinionated women."

> Smart Women Know: An intelligent
> man doesn't get nervous when a
> woman thinks for herself.

❦

*"A man can't stand a woman who
disagrees with him."*

> Smart Women Know: When a man
> loves you, he doesn't want you to
> turn into a wimp.

Smart Women Know That If You Try To
Please A Man By Behaving As Though You
Are Less Than You Are:

- You will start to believe that you *are* less than you are.

- You will end up resenting him.

- You will stunt your own growth, and you will limit the relationship.

Smart Women Know The Difference Between Fantasy And Reality.

No one would argue that fantasy, properly used, is not an important component in each of our lives. However sometimes a fantasy will give a woman unrealistic expectations or cause her to imagine that other women are having experiences that are more fulfilling. When that happens, fantasies can keep a woman from appreciating the reality that is her own life.

Smart Women Know . . .

It's human to always be a little dissatisfied, to wish that things were different, that you had more freedom, or more love, or more free time. It's human, but it's not very smart.

Smart Women Know . . .

How you fantasize about motherhood depends upon whether or not you are a mother.

- Childless professional women fantasize about cute little booties and rosy-cheeked toddlers in adorable snowsuits.

- Full-time, non-employed mothers fantasize about power lunches and fast-track wardrobes.

- Women with children *and* paying jobs fantasize about finding a clean blouse, an hour to themselves, and a decent night's sleep.

Smart Women Know . . .

    If You Try To Do It All At The Same Time, Then Something Is Going To Get Shortchanged—It Will Probably Be Your Needs.

Superwoman Is Super-Tired.

Smart Women Know What Is Wrong With These Pictures.

Do you remember seeing articles about "the superwoman," that spectacularly efficient creature who "has it all"? She lives an incredibly happy life in an incredibly beautiful home with her incredibly successful, supportive, and handsome husband and their two adorable tots. Her children are always happy, her job is always fulfilling, her husband is never resentful. She always looks oh-so-glamorous, color coordinated, and perfectly outfitted: When sharing quality time with her little ones, she is meticulously momlike in her white cashmere sweater, tan cashmere slacks, the gold bangles on her arm jingling as she pats her youngest on the head. When serving an exquisitely planned intimate dinner for six, she is gracefully elegant, not a spot on her little draped silk thing, the children tucked away for the night with nary a whimper. When heading for her high-powered corporate job, high in the tower suite of the highest building in town, her leather brief-

195

case at her side, she is properly suited for all forms of mergering and leveraging, not to mention quick trips to the coast.

Smart Women Know . . .
This woman doesn't exist.

Smart Women Know . . .

In the fantasy world, marriage is a solution to *everything*. In the real world, even the best marriages have conflicts and problems.

Even though you may have met someone with whom you want to share everything, it is entirely possible that you may disagree *vehemently* about:

- which movie to see

- which restaurant to eat in

- which television program to watch

- which music station to turn on

- where to go on vacation

- what to do on Friday night

Smart Women Know . . .

Once You Are Married, You And Your Spouse Will Have To Reach Compromises On The Following "Small" Issues:

- how warm the house stays in the winter

- how cool the air-conditioner gets turned on in the summer

- how far the windows get opened each night

- how soft or firm the mattress

- how many blankets go on the bed

- what time the lights go out in the bedroom at night

- what time the lights go on in the morning

- how often to have sex

Smart Women Know . . .

When you and your spouse go to a restaurant, no matter how much you love each other, you may not see eye to eye on:

- tipping

- sharing

- seating

- wine

- noise level

- paying

- dessert

Smart Women Know . . .

When You And The Man You Are With "For Better Or Worse" Are On Vacation, No Matter How Idyllic The Surroundings, You May Not Be In Perfect Accord On:

- who drives the car

- how fast it should be driven

- which hotel to stay in

- which sights to see

- when to stay

- when to leave

Smart Women Know . . .

If a couple tells you that they never argue, they are either lying or living in separate apartments.

Smart Women Know . . .

You can't have everything—at least not at the same time.

Within the last year, two of Mary Beth's closest friends got married; another two got engaged. Mary Beth wants to feel happy for them, but right now all she feels is envy. Mary Beth almost got married four years ago, but she broke it off because it "didn't feel right." Now, she is beginning to wonder if that was a mistake. When she was still in her twenties, not being married didn't upset her. But lately she has become depressed about being single. She is sure she would be a happy woman—if only she were married.

When Mary Beth thinks about marriage, she thinks about cozy nights by the fireplace, candlelit dinners for two, and chemistry that just won't quit. In fact, she has a whole repertoire of marriage fantasies. One of her favorites involves buying and decorating a house with her dream husband. Another one features idyllic vacations—snowy mountain slopes, summer houses, private beaches, European museums, a spontaneous weekend in New York, looking at autumn leaves in Vermont. Mary Beth also has "baby" daydreams. In them, she spends a lot of time shopping for "cute little things."

Her friends try to tell her that marriage is not quite what she imagines. They remind her that marriage is about compromise and that she likes to do things her way. They tell her that children and finances and work schedules get in the way of idyllic vacations. They tell her that babies get colic and cry, that babies get colds and cry, that babies get teeth and cry.

Mary Beth doesn't believe them. When her fantasy baby cries, it is only for a few minutes. And she is positive that once she is married, she and her husband will agree about everything. The way she looks at it, if she and a man love each other enough to get married, they will have two hearts that beat as one . . . two minds in perfect accord.

Cynthia has been married for five years. She loves her husband, and she knows he loves her . . . but certain things about marriage are making her crazy—like the way he throws his towels on the bed, and the fact that he never stays in one place, but always seems to be on the move through the house messing things up. And then there are his food habits—he can, and does, eat non-stop, never gaining weight, just creating garbage. He does his own dishes and all that, but even so, nothing is ever where she left it. And then, of course, sometimes he's downright cheap. He worries about money going "out the window" on heat, hot water, and electricity. They both fiddle with the thermostat so much it's a wonder it still works.

And lately their sex life has been for the birds. Between the kids and work, they're so tired that they both seem to have forgotten what desire feels like. The last vacation they took was a four-day weekend at the beach. It rained day and night. They did curl up in front of the fire, but instead of sharing their innermost thoughts, he watched the ball game and she read a terrific novel.

Cynthia doesn't want to be single again, but she remembers when she was and she remembers all the things she took for granted—such as sharing pizzas and Chinese food with friends, leaving dishes in the sink and not worrying about them, not having to account to anyone for anything, spending a weekend in bed curled up with her cat and watching movies nonstop. She remembers fun-filled weekends with friends learning how to ski; she remembers playing a Bangles tape and dancing naked in front of her bedroom mirror each morning before going to work; she remembers dressing up and looking forward to a date with a new man; she remembers shopping when she was the only person she had to spend money on; she remembers sex when she had a difficult time not thinking about it. She wishes she had known then how great it was to be single. She wishes she had been smart enough to enjoy her freedom, to make the most of it.

Smart Women Know . . .

Too many women ultimately feel as though they have wasted years of their lives dreaming about the future or lamenting the past; they would all agree that it's not smart.

Being smart requires living in the present and appreciating it for what it is.

Every day may not be the best of your life, but it is a day of your life so make the most of it.

Eleven Commandments For A Smart Woman

Thou shalt keep all thine expectations grounded in reality.

Thou shalt never forget thine priorities or thine sense of self.

Thou shalt not wait on any man more than he waits on you.

Thou shalt not wait for any man longer than he waits for you.

Thou shalt not spend more time analyzing any man's problems than you spend understanding your own.

Thou shalt not turn any mortal man into thine own personal god.

Thou shalt not covet thy neighbor's drama.

Thou shalt judge all men, not by their words, but by the consistency of their deeds.

Thou shalt not tolerate any form of abuse.

Thou shalt develop thine own talents, thine own potential, and thine own independence.

Thou shalt be fair to the men in thine life and expect fairness in return.

Smart Women Know . . .
It's Not Easy To Be Smart—But That
Shouldn't Keep You From Trying.